MAINTAINING THE PRIVACY OF LIBRARY RECORDS

A Handbook And Guide

Arlene Bielefield and Lawrence Cheeseman

Neal-Schuman Publishers, Inc.
New York   London

29954147

W9-DIG-832

Published by Neal-Schuman Publishers, Inc.
100 Varick Street
New York, NY 10013

Printed and bound in the United States of America

Library of Congress Cataloging-in-Publication Data

Bielefield , Arlene
    Maintaining the privacy of library records : a handbook and guide
  /   Arlene Bielefield and Lawrence Cheeseman.
        p.   cm.
    Includes bibliographical references and index.
    ISBN 1-55570-066-7 :
    1.   Confidential communications -- Library   records -- United States.
I.   Cheeseman , Lawrence. II. Title.
Z704.B54   1994
   025 . 5 ' 87-73 -- dc20   94 - 7153
                                                                        CIP

Contents

Acknowledgements

Introduction

In 1987 two agents of the Federal Bureau of Investigations visited the Math and Science Library of Columbia University. Their purpose was to enlist its librarians in a counter-intelligence program that later came to be known as the FBI Awareness Program. From additional visits to other libraries it became apparent that the FBI's purpose was to find out how specific individuals were using the library or who in general was accessing scientific and technical information. In some cases the FBI agents were just asking if any suspicious activities had occurred recently in the library.[1] Representative Don Edwards, chair of the House of Representatives, Subcommittee on Civil and Constitutional Rights, Committee on the Judiciary concluded that: "The FBI apparently assumes that the threat of KGB collection of unclassified information available to U.S. libraries is sufficiently great, and the payoff from their efforts in libraries so significant that they outweigh any unintended chilling effect on the life of mind."[2] The reaction of the library community was firm and resolute. The FBI's activities were a wake-up call to everyone in the library community that the confidentiality of library records cannot be taken for granted. Library organizations and librarians individually made it clear that they would not voluntarily cooperate with the FBI or any other government agency in monitoring library use or users. It was clear that the library community feared that word of such cooperation would frighten library users and discourage them from exercising their rights to use the library.

At a Congressional hearing on the program, the library community—including the Special Libraries Association, American Library Association, and the Association of Research Libraries—advanced many arguments against cooperating with this program. Many pointed out that there were serious constitutional issues involved and that to assist in such activities violated the laws of many states.

Purpose

This handbook is a practical guide to the constitutional issues, federal laws, and state statutes governing the privacy of library records. Its basic supposition is that the only way to fully protect the confidentiality of library records is to practice defensive law—avoiding legal problems by anticipating and taking affirmative steps to avoid them. These steps are understanding the legal and constitutional issues involved, and developing a library policy that is understood and practiced by all library staff.

Organization

This book is divided into three parts. Part I deals with federal protection of the confidentiality of library records. Understanding the constitutional issues involved in the privacy of library records is essential. Part I also covers federal laws concerning the confidentiality of records and the attempt to pass a national law. Each chapter begins with a series of questions that provide the focus of discussion.

Part II contains a state-by-state compilation and analysis of laws protecting library records. Part III presents a sample library policy on the confidentiality of library records.

Warning

It should always be remembered that protecting the confidentiality of library use and users is an ongoing, never-ending task. Threats to privacy are usually very subtle: An offer by a vendor to reduce the library's subscription to its service if the vendor can maintain a log of users involves profound constitutional and legal issues. What the U.S. Supreme Court said of the First Amendment can also be said of the privacy of library records:

The fundamental freedom of speech and press have contributed greatly to the development and well-being of our free society and are indispensable to its continued growth. Ceaseless vigilance is the watchword to prevent their erosion by Congress or by the States. The door barring federal and state intrusions into this area cannot be left ajar; it must be kept tightly closed and opened only the slightest crack necessary to prevent encroachment upon more important interests.[3]

The library community must always remain vigilant.

Notes

1. See testimony of Duane E. Webster, Executive Director of the Association of Research Libraries, in *Hearings Before the Subcommittee on Civil and Constitutional Rights of the Committee on the Judiciary*, Serial No. 123, 100th Cong., 2d Sess.(June 20 and July 13, 1988), p.7.
2. *Hearings Before the Subcommittee on Civil and Constitutional Rights of the Committee on the Judiciary*, p.6.
3. *Roth v. United States*, 354 U.S. 476 at 488(1957).

PART I

Federal Protection of the Privacy of Library Records

1
The First Amendment

- *Does the First Amendment to the Constitution guarantee the confidentiality of library records?*
- *Are First Amendment rights absolute and inviolable?*
- *What were the motivating forces behind the adoption of the First Amendment so soon after the Constitution was ratified?*
- *Are there any peripheral rights in the First Amendment that relate to libraries?*

Americans react automatically and with very strong feelings to any attempt to abridge or violate the rights and freedoms guaranteed by the First Amendment. This is because these rights are central to our concept of liberty.[1] For this reason our most immediate reaction to the question about the confidentiality of library records is that these records must be protected by the First Amendment. All inquiries into the confidentiality of library records must thus begin, with the First Amendment, the most fundamental personal rights protected by the Constitution.

In this chapter we will consider whether First Amendment guarantees are broad enough to protect the confidentiality of library records. To determine this, we will first have to look carefully at the First Amendment's history, language, and purposes, and see how each of these has been interpreted and applied by the United States Supreme Court.[2]

HISTORY OF THE FIRST AMENDMENT

The First Amendment was not part of the U. S. Constitution as it was originally drafted in Philadelphia by the Constitutional Convention during the summer of 1787. In the closing days of that convention, several proposals to add a bill of rights were voted down with

3

relatively little discussion. While the exact reasons are not known for sure, many delegates may have felt that a national bill of rights was simply unnecessary because the new federal government did not have any powers that would make it necessary to have such prohibitions. Some delegates may have feared that a bill of rights would just add to the controversy already surrounding the Constitution just as it was being submitted to the states for ratification. Other delegates may have been mindful of the late hour.

After the U. S. Constitution was finally signed by the delegates on September 17, 1787, and submitted to the states for ratification, the lack of a bill of rights drew more public criticism than any other aspect of the Constitution. There are several reasons for this:

1. The early colonists regarded these freedoms and rights to be part of their English heritage,[3] derived from British law[4] and political philosophy.[5]
2. Prior to the drafting of the Constitution several states had even adopted a bill of rights in their own state constitutions.[6] For example, 10 of the 14 states that ratified the Constitution—Delaware, Georgia, Maryland, Massachusetts, New Hampshire, North Carolina, Pennsylvania, South Carolina, Vermont, and Virginia—had provisions guaranteeing freedom of expression.[7]
3. There was a deep distrust of the powers being concentrated in a federal government. Many feared the return of the restraints imposed upon the colonists by the British government to prevent the Revolution. [8] Especially feared were restraints on freedom of religion, press, assembly, and speech.[9]
4. A strong case was made for the argument that a government of limited power need not be an anemic government. Assuring citizens that their rights are secure tends to diminish the fear of strong government and encourages their support.[10]

It thus became clear that the Constitution would not be ratified by the states without a firm assurance from its drafters that a bill of rights would be approved in the form of amendments to the new Constitution at the very first session of Congress.[11] The promise was made and the Constitution was ratified by the required nine states on June 21, 1788, with the understanding that the new Congress would draft and recommend to the states the adoption of such a bill of rights.

At that first session of Congress, the House of Representatives adopted 17 proposed amendments to the Constitution. The Senate[12] reduced that number to twelve, which was then agreed to by the House and sent on to the states for ratification on September 25, 1789. Ten of the 12 amendments were ratified by 11 of the 14 states and added to the Constitution on December 15, 1791. The two rejected amendments had to do with the number of representatives to Congress and the compensation that was due to the senators and representatives. The First Amendment was so named because it was the first one to be accepted.

LANGUAGE OF THE FIRST AMENDMENT

The United States Constitution, Amendment I, states: Congress shall make no law respecting an establishment of religion, or prohibiting the free exercise thereof; or abridging the freedom of speech, or of the press; or the right of the people peaceably to assemble, and to petition the Government for a redress of grievances.

Applicability

The first word, "Congress," would seem to limit the prohibitions of the First Amendment to the federal government. However, the Fourteenth Amendment[13] to the Constitution, which was ratified in 1868, was determined by the U. S. Supreme Court in 1925[14] to make the rights in the First Amendment applicable to the states and, through them, to all of their political subdivisions-counties, cities, towns, villages, and boroughs.

Unequivocal

The phrase "shall make no law" would appear to be mandatory, absolute, and without exceptions or limitations. "No" should after all mean no. In actuality, Congress has never accepted the First Amendment prohibitions as either absolute or inviolate. In 1798, just seven years after it became part of the Constitution, Congress enacted the Sedition Act. This act punished anyone who would

> write, print, utter or publish . . . any false, scandalous and malicious writing or writings against the government of the United States, or either house of the Congress of the United States, or of the President of the United States, with intent to defame the said government, or either house of the said Congress, or the said President, or to bring them, or either of them, into contempt or disrepute. . . .[15]

Many, including Thomas Jefferson, believed the statutes clearly violated the First Amendment.[16] In 1940 Congress enacted the Alien Registration Act (Smith Act), and in 1950, the Subversive Control Act

(McCarran Act). These acts violated the absolute prohibition against the enactment of laws limiting freedom of speech.

The U. S. Supreme Court has never regarded the freedoms of the First Amendment as absolute. Appendix A contains excerpts from U. S. Supreme Court opinions, arranged chronologically, setting forth the exceptions and limitations to the First Amendment. Why would the Court and the Congress so steadfastly stand against what is clearly the plain and simple meaning of the First Amendment? There are several reasons:

1. Exceptions had always been recognized for the Bill of Rights, even by the drafters of the Constitution and its amendments.[17] For example, the Second Amendment guarantee of the right to bear arms never was intended to include the right to carry concealed weapons. The Fifth Amendment prohibition against being put in jeopardy twice does not prevent a second trial if the jury in the first trial fails to agree. Nor does the Fifth Amendment provision that no one shall be a witness against him/herself prevent that testimony if a prosecution is barred by a pardon or the lapsing of a statute of limitation.[18]

2. An absolute, unequivocal right without limitations or exceptions would not work. The Bill of Rights appears at the end of a constitution that sets up a federal government; and it clearly is not intended to replace it or to render it unworkable. Without a society capable of maintaining public order, liberty would be lost in the excesses of anarchy.[19]

3. An extreme, uncompromising position would lead to irreconcilable conflict between several of the clauses in the First Amendment itself.

While the absolutist position has never been accepted by the full court, two justices, Justice Hugo L. Black and William O. Douglas, held that the First Amendment means just what it says, and they expressed this view in dissenting opinions. Justice Black was the most consistent advocate of the absolutist position. In a 1952 case, he stated: "I do not agree that the Constitution leaves freedom of petition, assembly, speech, press or worship at the mercy of a case-by-case, day-by-day majority of this Court. . . . I think the First Amendment with the Fourteenth 'absolutely' forbids such laws without 'ifs' or 'buts' or 'whereases.'"[20]

Justice Douglas was not as consistent in his support of the absolutist position. In a 1973 case, he noted in his dissenting opinion: "The First Amendment is written in terms that are absolute. Its command is that 'Congress shall make no law . . . abridging the freedom of speech or of the press. . . .' The ban of 'no' law that abridges freedom of the press is in my view total and complete."[21] However, Justice Douglas did not hold this view in all instances. In 1950 he stated in a dissenting opinion: "The freedom to speak is not absolute."[22] In 1966, in another dissenting opinion, he recognized that there is a time, place, and manner limitation on freedom of speech: "No one, for example, would suggest that the Senate gallery is the proper place for a vociferous protest rally."[23]

Rights and Liberties

The remainder of the text of the First Amendment concerns three fundamental and interconnected rights: freedom from government interference in religion, expression (speech and press), and assembly and petition. These rights are fundamental liberties, essential to the pursuit of happiness. They are the very rights and freedoms that the *Declaration of Independence* declares to be inalienable and the reasons for which governments are instituted.[24]

Religion

"Congress shall make no law respecting an establishment of religion, or prohibiting the free exercise thereof. . . ."[25] This creates two distinct prohibitions: one relating to the "establishment" of religion and the other to the "free exercise" of religion. The first prohibition, which has come to be known as the Establishment Clause, has the practical effect of excluding the federal government and the states from acting in the area of religion. Federal and state governments must remain neutral in matters of religion. They may not set up a church, pass laws that aid one religion, aid all religions, or prefer one religion over another.[26] They cannot levy a tax to support any religious activity or openly or secretly participate in the affairs of any religious organizations.[27] In Jefferson's words, the clause was intended to erect "a wall of separation between church and state."[28] The second prohibition, known as the Free Exercise Clause, bars the regulation by government of religious beliefs as such. It prohibits government from discrimination against individuals or groups because of their religious views or beliefs, and government cannot compel individuals to affirm any particular religious belief in conflict with their own.[29]

Both the Establishment and Free Exercise Clauses resulted from the American Colonists' experiences with government-supported religions. Many of the early settlers came from Europe to escape laws that compelled them to support and attend government favored churches. They saw firsthand the turmoil, civil strife, and persecutions that came about in part because established religious sects were determined to maintain their absolute political and religious supremacy. In 1947 the court stated: "In efforts to force loyalty to whatever religious group happened to be on top and in league with the government of a particular time and place, men and women had been fined, cast in jail, cruelly tortured, and killed."[30]

Offenses that were this severely punished included speaking disrespectfully of the views of ministers of government-established churches, nonattendance at those churches, expressions of nonbelief, and the failure to pay taxes to support those churches.

Even in the New World these practices continued. The very charters granted by the English Crown authorized religious establishments which all, including non-believers, must support and attend. Colonists who happened to be in the minority in a particular locality were persecuted because they steadfastly held to worshipping only as their own consciences dictated. These practices were so commonplace that they created the conviction that individual religious liberty could be achieved best under a government that was stripped of all power to tax, support, or assist any or all religions, or to interfere with the beliefs of any religious individual or group.[31]

In addition to persecutions, the union of government and religion tends to destroy government and to degrade religion. The history of government-established religion, both in England and in America, shows that whenever government has allied itself with one particular religion, the inevitable result has been the display of hatred, disrespect, and even contempt toward those who held contrary beliefs. History also shows that many people have lost their respect for any religion that relies upon the support of government to spread its faith.[32]

As with the other freedoms guaranteed under the First Amendment, the Court has not interpreted or applied the religion clauses in the absolute terms in which they are written. One cannot, for example, refuse to testify in court because of religious beliefs, even if it violates the tenets of his or her faith.[33] A religious congregation cannot violate a local zoning ordinance that prohibits construction of church buildings in residential districts, even if it means the congregation cannot construct a building on a lot it owns.[34] In addition, The Court has held that government can prevent or punish religious activity in the face of clear and present danger of riot, disorder, interference with traffic upon public streets, or immediate threats to public safety, peace, or order.[35]

The Court has also struggled to find a neutral course between the two clauses; if carried to their logical extreme, they would clash with one another. For example, paying an army chaplin with federal funds might be said to violate the Establishment Clause. However, soldiers stationed at a faraway outpost could complain that a government that did not provide a chaplain was preventing them from participating in the free exercise of their religion.[36] Rigidity would thus thwart the basic function of these Clauses.[37]

It is clear that Americans will not tolerate either government-established religion or government interference with religion.[38] Short of these prohibitions, however, the Court has sought to find room for neutrality. In 1952 the court said: "The First Amendment . . . does not say that in every and all respects there shall be a separation of Church and State."[39] Indeed, as a practical matter there can be no such complete and uncompromising separation.In 1947 the Court upheld a state statute that reimbursed the parents of parochial school children for bus transportation expenses,[40]

In 1968 the Court upheld the state loans of textbooks to parochial schools.[41] In 1952 the Court approved the release during school hours of pupils to go to religious centers for religious instructions.[42]

However, four years earlier, the Court had voided a program establishing a period during which pupils in public schools were to be allowed to receive religious instructions.[43] The difference turned on the programs being conducted off school property.

In cases involving a conflict between secular interests and religious rights, the court has followed a policy of determining whether the government's purpose is sufficiently compelling and whether the means the government chooses to achieve that goal have been narrowly tailored to respect those religious rights.[44] The Court also tests to see if the law has a secular legislative purpose, if the law's primary effect advances or inhibits religion, and if the law fosters an excessive government entanglement with religion.[45]

In regard to the Free Exercise Clause, the Court has also attempted to draw a distinction between belief and conduct. The freedom to believe is absolute, but the freedom to act may be limited. A state or local government can by general and nondiscriminatory legislation regulate the time, place, and manner of conduct and may in other ways safeguard the peace, order, and comfort of the community without unconstitutionally invading the beliefs of its citizens.[46] The Free Exercise Clause does not include the right to violate statutory laws or maintain a nuisance. the court has stated that, "the fact that one acts from the promptings of religious beliefs does not immunize against lawless conduct."[47]

Expression

The clause stating, "Congress shall make no laws . . . abridging the freedom of speech, or of the press," was introduced into the House of Representatives on June 8, 1789, as: "The people shall not be deprived or abridged of their right to speak, to write, or to publish their sentiments; and the freedom of the press, as one of the great bulwarks of liberty, shall be inviolable."[48] In the Senate it was amended and given its final form. It is unclear from the records of the Constitutional Convention or from the debate in the House as to what the real purposes were behind this clause. There is no record of any debate in the Senate or in the states during ratification. The reason for the lack of debate may be that the Amendment was not seen as a novel principle of government but rather as the continuation of rights guaranteed by English law and tradition.[49]

Because of this the Court has been required to identify the purposes behind the Speech and Press Clause. One of the most important and unquestioned[50] of these purposes is to insure "unfettered interchange of ideas for the bringing about of political and social changes desired by the people."[51] The opportunity for free political discussion must be maintained so that government will be responsible to the will of the people and that changes may be obtained by lawful means.[52] Under the British rule, the Crown was sovereign and the people were subjects. Under the Constitution, it is the people, not the government that possesses the absolute sovereignty. The power to censor must be exercised by the people over government, not in government over the people.

The Speech and Press Clause also presupposes that truth is more likely to emerge from a multitude of tongues than through any kind of authoritative pronouncement. Justice Holmes believed that the "best test of truth is the power of the thought to get itself accepted in the competition of the market. . . ."[53] It is for this reason that debate on public issues should be uninhibited, robust, and wide-open, and may well include vehement, caustic, and sometimes unpleasant attacks.[54] Such freedom imposes obvious risks to government institutions, but it is far more hazardous to discourage thought. The safest path is not through repression but through the opportunity to discuss freely grievances and remedies.[55]

There are also purposes behind the Speech and Press Clause of the Constitution that more directly affect individuals. In a 1927 concurring opinion, Justices Brandeis and Holmes gave those purposes a classic formulation that deserves to be quoted in full:

> Those who won our independence believed that the final end of the State was to make men free to develop their faculties; and that in its government the deliberative forces should prevail over the arbitrary. They believed that freedom to think as you will and to speak as you think are means indispensable to the discovery and spread of political truth; that without free speech and assembly discussion would be futile; that with them, discussion affords ordinarily adequate protection against the dissemination of noxious doctrine; that the greatest menace to freedom is an inert people. . . .[56]

The purposes of the Speech and Press Clause thus include self-actualization (the freedom to develop your faculties), liberty(both as an end and a means), truth (the freedom to think and to speak are indispensable to finding the truth), and freedom to change (inertia is the greatest enemy).

The Court has not interpreted or applied the Speech and Press Clauses in the absolute terms in which it is written. Freedom of speech and of the press does not confer an absolute right to speak or publish without responsibility. For example, it does not mean that anyone with an opinion or belief may address a group at any public place and at any time.[57] No one can ignore a red light as a means of social protest, and no one would defend a street meeting in the middle of Times Square at rush hour as a form of freedom of speech.

Limitations and exceptions were recognized by the drafters of the clauses. Libel and obscenity were never envisioned to be within the scope of constitutionally protected speech. Obscenity was excluded because it was viewed as having nothing to do with the unfettered interchange of ideas for bringing about political or social changes.[58] It was not considered essential for the exposition of ideas and was of such slight social value that any benefit derived from it was outweighed by the social interest in order and morality.[59]

Despite these limitations, the practical effect of the Speech and Press Clause is to bar most prior restraint of expression. It also limits subsequent punishment to a very narrow range of expression.

Press

In early America, freedom of the press meant immunity from prior restraint or censorship.[60] Under the English system all printers were licensed and nothing could be published without the prior approval of the state or the church. The great struggle for freedom of the press was thus for the right to publish without a license.[61]

The purpose of the Press Clause was stated in a 1774 letter of the Continental Congress to the inhabitants of Quebec:

> The last right we shall mention regards the freedom of the press. The importance of this consists, besides the advancement of truth, science, morality, and arts in general, in its diffusion of liberal sentiments on the administration of Government, its ready communication of thoughts between subjects, and its consequential promotion of union among them, whereby oppressive officers are shamed or intimidated, into more honorable and just modes of conducting affairs.[62]

The Court thus acknowledged the role of the press to scrutinize the conduct of public affairs and has made it clear that just because freedom of the press can be abused does not make it any less necessary. Subsequent punishment for abuses, not prior restraint, is the appropriate remedy.[63] Only in exceptional circumstances is prior restraint permitted. The only discretion that public officials should have in issuing permits should be related to questions of time, place, and manner.[64]

Assembly and Petition

"Congress shall make no law . . . abridging . . . the right of the people peaceably to assemble, and to petition the Government for a redress of grievances." These rights are closely related in origin and purpose with the rights of free speech and free press. Like the Speech and Press Clause, the purpose of this clause is to assure freedom of communication on matters related to the functioning of government.[65] The very idea of government in America implies a right of citizens to meet peaceably to discuss and consult on public affairs and to petition the government for a redress of grievances.[66] It was thus not by accident or coincidence that the clauses were coupled. Freedom of speech and of the press and the right to assemble and petition are inseparable rights or, in the words of the Court, they are "cognate rights."[67]

The right of petition existed long before the Constitution. It was deeply rooted in the English tradition. The right can be traced to the *Magna Carta* of 1215 and it appeared in the English Bill of Rights of 1689.[68] Even before the Constitutional Convention, the right of petition appeared in the Declaration of Rights of several state constitutions including that of Pennsylvania.[69] Under prior English law, however, the right to assemble was considered to be merely instrumental to the right of petition. In the First Amendment, the two rights are made equally fundamental. Under the First Amendment and in the view of the Court, neither right can be denied without violating the fundamental principles of liberty and justice that are at the base of all civil and political institutions.[70]

These rights are also not limited to religious and political grievances. The right to assemble, for example, protects the right to discuss and inform people of the advantages and disadvantages of unions.[71] The right of petition for redress of grievances is not limited to just government officials and legislatures but also includes the courts.[72] Nor is it limited to a redress for grievances alone; it also includes the right to demand that government use its powers to further the interests of the petitioners and of their views on politically contentious matters.[73]

Like other First Amendment rights, however, the right to assemble and to petition is not absolute. It is limited in the same way as freedom of speech and of the press. For example, they offer no immunity from damages for libel.[74] The Court has, however, made it clear that any attempt to limit these liberties must be justified by a clear public interest that is being threatened by a clear and present danger. If a discussion is orderly and at an appropriate time and place, only such a real or impending danger can be used to justify its limitation. In the Court's view, there must be the widest room for discussion and the narrowest range for its restriction.[75] Mere public intolerance or animosity is not enough. In the opinion of the Court, "The First and Fourteenth Amendments do not permit a State to make criminal the exercise of the right of assembly simply because its exercise may be 'annoying' to some people."[76] After all, debate on public issues should be uninhibited, robust, and wide open.[77]

ADDITIONAL RIGHTS

In addition to the rights specifically enumerated in the language of the First Amendment, there are others which the Court has recognized as being essential, although not specifically mentioned. These peripheral rights are described by the Court by a term associated with eclipses and sunspots. The dark area of an eclipse or sunspot is called the umbra. The area between this absolute dark area and the full light is an area of partial shadow known as the penumbra. In the 1965 case of *Griswold v. Connecticut*,[78] the Court stated that the specific guarantees in the First Amendment and in the rest of the Bill of Rights have penumbras. These penumbral rights are formed by emanations from the specific guarantees, and it is those specific guarantees that give penumbral rights their life and substance.

The confidentiality of library records is not guaranteed by any explicitedly enumerated right in the First Amendment, although it is clear from the history, purpose, and interpretation of the First Amendment that there are reasonable grounds for supposing such protection. There are, however, three penumbral rights that emanate from the First Amendment that do relate more directly to library records. The first of these is the constitutional right to receive information and ideas. This right is treated in chapter 2. The constitutional right of association and the constitutional right to privacy, are discussed in chapter 3.

Notes

1. As the United States Supreme Court stated in 1920: "That freedom of speech and of the press are elements of liberty all will acclaim. Indeed they are so intimate to liberty in every one's convictions—we may say feelings—that there is an instinctive and instant revolt from any limitation of them by law. . . ." *Schaefer v. United States*, 251 U.S. 466 at 474 (1920).
2. In *Marbury v. Madison*, 5 U.S. 137(1803), the Court held that it had the constitutional power to strike down state or federal statutes that violate the U.S. Constitution.
3. *Robertson v. Baldwin*, 165 U.S. 275 at 281 (1897).
4. These guaranteed freedoms can be found in documents such as the Magna Carta(1215), in English statutes such as the Bill of Rights(1689), and in the numerous decisions of the English courts, as well as in the unwritten English Constitution itself.
5. In British philosophy these rights were expressed by John Locke, whose ideas formed the basis of the *Declaration of Independence*.
6. For example, Virginia Bill of Rights (June 12, 1776), Article 1, states, "That all men are by nature equally free and independent, and have certain inherent rights, of which, when they enter into a state of society, they cannot by any compact deprive or divest their posterity; namely, the enjoyment of life and liberty, with the means of acquiring and possessing property, and pursuing and obtaining happiness and safety."
7. *Roth v. United States*, 354 U.S. 476 at 482(1957).
8. *Commonwealth v. Blanding*, 20 Mass. 304 at 313(1825).
9. *New York Times Co. v. United States*, 403 U.S. 713 at 715-716. In introducing the Bill of Rights to the House of Representatives, Madison said that he believed that the "great mass of the people who oppose [the Constitution], disliked it because it did not contain effectual provisions against the encroachments on particular rights. . . ." 1 *Annals of Congress* 433.

10. *West Virginia State Board of Education v. Barnett*, 319 U.S. 624 at 636-637(1943).
11. Ibid. at 637.
12. One of the amendments rejected by the Senate reads: "The equal rights of conscience, the freedom of speech or of the press, and the right of trial by jury in criminal cases shall not be infringed by any State." James Madison declared that this amendment was "the most valuable of the whole list." *Annals of Congress* 755(August 17, 1789). The restrictions of the First Amendment were not declared to apply to the states by the U.S. Supreme Court until 1925.
13. The specific clause was, "nor shall any State deprive any person of life, liberty, or property, without due process of law. . . ."
14. "For present purposes we may and do assume that freedom of speech and of the press—which are protected by the First Amendment from abridgment by Congress—are among the fundamental personal rights and 'liberties' protected by the due process clause of the Fourteenth Amendment from impairment by the States." *Gitlow v. New York*, 268 U.S. 652 at 666 (1925).
15. Sedition Act of 1789, 1 Stat. 596, sec.2.
16. Supreme Court Justice Douglas, in 1973 also thought the acts were unconstitutional. *Columbia Broadcasting v. Democratic Committee*, 412 U.S. 94 at 156 (1973).
17. *Robertson* at 281. Consider also Justice Frankfurter's concurring opinion in *Dennis v. United States*(1951): ". . . there are those who find in the Constitution a wholly unfettered right of expression. Such literalness treats the words of the Constitution as though they were found on a piece of outworn parchment instead of being words that have called into being a nation with a past to be preserved for the future. The soil in which the Bill of Rights grew was not a soil of arid pedantry. The historic antecedents of the First Amendment preclude the notion that its purpose was to give unqualified immunity to every expression that touched on matters within the range of political interest." 341 U.S. 494 at 521 (1951).
18. *Robertson* at 282.
19. *Cox v. Louisiana*, 379 U.S. 536 at 554(1965).
20. *Beauharnais v. Illinois*, 343 U.S. 250 at 274-275 (1952). Dissenting opinion.
21. *Columbia Broadcasting* at 156 (1973).
22. *Dennis* at 581 (1950).
23. *Adderley v. Florida*, 385 U.S. 39 at 54 (1966).
24. The exact words were: "We hold these truths to be self-evident, that all men are created equal, that they are endowed by their Creator with certain unalienable Rights, that among these are Life, Liberty, and the pursuit of Happiness . . . That to secure these rights, Governments are instituted among Men, deriving their just powers from the consent of the governed, That whenever any Form of Government becomes destructive of these ends, it is the Right of the People to alter or to abolish it, and to institute new Government, laying its foundation on such principles and

organizing its powers in such form, as to them shall seem most likely to effect their Safety and Happiness."

25. The original language of the First Amendment clause relating to religion was, "The civil rights of none shall be abridged on account of religious belief or worship, nor shall any national religion be established, nor shall the full and equal right of conscience be in any manner, or any pretense, infringed." *Annals of Congress* 434(June 8, 1789). The current language was adopted in the Senate and House Conference.
26. *Everson v. Board of Education*, 330 U.S. 1 at 15(1947).
27. Ibid. at 15-16.
28. Ibid.
29. *Braunfield v. Brown*, 366 U.S. 599(1961).
30. *Everson* at 9.
31. Ibid. at 11.
32. *Engel v. Vitale*, 370 U.S. 421 at 431(1962).
33. *State v. Bing*, 253 S.E.2d 101 at 102(1979).
34. *Lakewood, Ohio Congregation of Jehovah's Witnesses, Inc., v. City of Lakewood*, Ohio, 699 F.2d 303 at 305(1983).
35. *Cantwell v. Connecticut*, 310 U.S. 300 at 304(1940).
36. This example is used by Justice Stewart in his dissenting opinion in *Sherbert v. Verner*, 374 U.S. 398.
37. *Walz v. Tax Commission*, 397 U.S. 664 at 669(1970).
38. In *West Virginia State Board of Education* at 642, the Court said, "If there is any fixed star in our constitutional constellation, it is that no official, high or petty, can prescribe what shall be orthodox in politics, nationalism, religion, or other matters of opinion. . . ."
39. *Zorach v. Clauson*, 343 U.S. 306 at 312(1952).
40. *Everson* at 1.
41. *Board of Education v. Allen*, 392 U.S. 236 at 243 (1968).
42. *Zorach* at 306.
43. *Illinois ex rel. McCollum v. Board of Education*, 333 U.S. 203(1948).
44. *Africa v. Anderson*, 542 F.Supp. 224 at 228(1982). In *Cantwell* at p. 304, the Court stated: "In every case the power to regulate must be so exercised as not, in attaining a permissible end, unduly to infringe the protected freedom."
45. *Lemon v. Kurtzman*, 403 U.S. 602 at 612-3(1971).
46. *Cantwell*, p. 304.
47. *State ex rel. Swann v. Pack*, 527 S.W. 2d 99 at 111(1975). Affirmed by the U.S. Supreme Court at 424 U.S. 954(1975).
48. 1 *Annals of Congress* 434(1789).
49. 165 U.S. 275 at 281 (1897).
50. In *Mills v. Alabama*, 384 U.S. 214 at 219(1966) the Court stated: "Whatever differences may exist about interpretations of the First Amendment, there is practically universal agreement that a major purpose of that Amendment was to protect the free discussion of governmental affairs."

51. *Roth v. United States*, 354 U.S. 476 at 484(1957).
52. *Stromberg v. California*, 283 U.S. 359 at 369(1931).
53. Justice Holmes' dissenting opinion in *Abrams v. United States*, 250 U.S. 616 at 630(1919).
54. *Terminiello v. Chicago*, 337 U.S. 1 at 4(1949).
55. In 1927, Justice Brandeis in a concurring opinion to *Whitney v. California*, 274 U.S. 357 at 375-376, gave this argument a classic formulation: "Those who won our independence believed . . . that public discussion is a political duty; and that this should be a fundamental principle of the American government. They recognized the risks to which all human institutions are subject. But they knew that order cannot be secured merely through fear of punishment for its infraction; that it is hazardous to discourage thought, hope and imagination; that fear breeds repression; that repression breeds hate; that hate menaces stable government; that the path to safety lies in the opportunity to discuss freely supposed grievances and proposed remedies; and the fitting remedy for evil counsels is good ones. Believing in the power of reason as applied through public discussion, they eschewed silence coerced by law—the argument of force in its worst form. Recognizing the occasional tyrannies of governing majorities, they amended the Constitution so that free speech and assembly should be guaranteed."
56. *Whitney* at 375(1927).
57. *Cox v. Louisiana*, 379 U.S. 536 at 554(1965).
58. *Roth* at 484.
59. *Chaplinsky v. New Hampshire*, 315 U.S. 568 at 571-572(1942).
60. *Near v. Minnesota ex rel. Olson*, 283 U.S. 697 at 716(1931).
61. Ibid. at 713-714.
62. 1 *Journals of the Continental Congress* 108(1774) quoted in *Roth* at 484.
63. As stated in *Near* at pp.719-720:"[T]he administration of government has become more complex, the opportunities for malfeasance and corruption have multiplied, crime has grown to most serious proportions, and the danger of its protection by unfaithful officials and of the impairment of the fundamental security of life and property by criminal alliances and official neglect, emphasizes the primary need of a vigilant and courageous press, especially in great cities. The fact that the liberty of the press may be abused by miscreant purveyors of scandal does not make any the less necessary the immunity of the press from previous restraint in dealing with official misconduct. Subsequent punishment for such abuses as may exist is the appropriate remedy, consistent with constitutional privilege."
64. *Cox v. New Hampshire*, 312 U.S. 569(1941).
65. *Richmond Newspapers, Inc. v. Virginia*, 448 U.S. 555 at 575(1980).
66. *De Jonge v. State of Oregon*, 299 U.S. 353 at 552-553(1937).
67. *Thomas v. Collins*, 323 U.S. 516 at 530(1945).
68. "[I]t is the Right of the Subjects to petition the King." Wm. & Mary, Sess 2, ch 2.

69. *McDonald v. Smith*, 472 U.S. 479 at 483-484(1985).
70. *DeJonge* at 364-365.
71. *Thomas* at 531.
72. Rhem v. McGrath, 326 F.Supp 681 at 680(1971).
73. *Eastern R.R. Presidents Conference v. Noerr Motor Freight*, 365 U.S. 127(1961).
74. *McDonald v. Smith*, 472 U.S. 479 at 483(1985).
75. *Thomas* at 530.
76. *Coates v. Cincinnati*, 402 U.S. 611 at 615(1971).
77. *New York Times Co.* at 270.
78. 381 U.S. 479.

2
Constitutional Right to Receive Information and Ideas

- *Where can the Constitutional right to receive information and ideas be found?*
- *Why is this right particularly important to libraries?*
- *Does the right protect the confidentiality of library records?*
- *What is the relationship between the Federal Freedom of Information Act and this right?*

The First Amendment of the Constitution declares that "Congress shall make no laws . . . abridging the freedom of speech, or of the press. . . ." The right to receive information and ideas is founded under this prohibition. While not actually mentioned in the words of the clause, this right is so essential to the amendment's fullest exercise that it must be considered a necessary penumbral right.

For libraries, the constitutional right to receive information and ideas is one of the most important penumbral rights. This right confirms that the First Amendment does more than prohibit government from enacting laws that censor information. The First Amendment also encompasses a positive right of public access to information and ideas. In 1992 the Third Circuit U.S. Court of Appeals stated that this penumbral right "includes the right to some level of access to a public library, the quintessential locus of the receipt of information."[1] A court case involving libraries also figures prominently in the development of the right itself.

In this chapter we will consider whether the constitutional right to receive information and ideas protects the confidentiality of library records. To determine this we will first have to look carefully at the development of this right. Like other rights under the First Amendment, recognition of the right to receive information and ideas can be traced historically through the opinions of the United States Supreme Court.

HISTORICAL DEVELOPMENT

1943

In *Martin v. City of Struthers*[2] the Court decided for the first time that freedom to speak also included the right to receive speech. This case dealt with the constitutionality of a municipal ordinance of the city of Struthers, Ohio, which forbids any person from knocking on the door, ringing the doorbell, or otherwise summoning the occupants of any residence for the purpose of distributing handbills or circulars to them. The purpose of the ordinance was to protect residents from annoyance and to prevent crime. Struthers was at that time an industrial community, in which most residents worked in the iron and steel industry. Many worked on swing shifts, working nights, and sleeping days. In addition, it was noted that burglars often posed as canvassers in order to discover if a house was empty or to determine which one to rob.

Ms. Martin, a Jehovah's Witness, admitted distributing leaflets about a meeting of her religious group by knocking at doors in the city in violation of the ordinance. Even though she had proceeded in a conventional and orderly fashion, she was convicted in the Mayor's Court and fined $10.00. She appealed her conviction, arguing that the ordinance was unconstitutional. The Court agreed: "The authors of the First Amendment knew that novel and unconventional ideas might disturb the complacent, but they chose to encourage a freedom which they believed essential if vigorous enlightenment was ever to triumph over slothful ignorance."[3]

While this freedom embraces the right to distribute literature, the Court noted that it also *"necessarily protects the right to receive it."*[4] [emphasis added].

In this case, the Court weighed three interests against each other: 1) Ms. Martin's interest in distributing information, 2) residents' interest in choosing whether to receive that information, and 3) the city's interest in protecting its citizens, whether they want that protection or not.

The Court viewed the city's interest in this ordinance as involving the substitution of its judgment for the judgment of the individual resident. Ms. Martin was convicted of a crime for annoying people on whom she called, even though some of those residents were, in fact, glad to receive her flyers.[5]

A less intrusive means can and should be found to accomplish the ordinance's purpose, one that would protect the rights of those desiring to distribute literature, those wishing to receive it, and those who wish to exclude such distribution from their homes.[6] In the view of the Court, "Freedom to distribute information to every citizen wherever he desires to receive it is so clearly vital to the preservation of a free society that, putting aside reasonable police and health regulations of time and manner of distribution, it must be fully preserved."[7] The dangers the ordinances wished to avoid can easily be controlled by other legal methods. In this way each householder can have the full right to decide whether he or she will receive strangers as visitors. The Court ruled that the ordinance served no purpose "but that forbidden by the Constitution, the naked restriction of the dissemination of ideas."[8]

May 1965

In *Lamont v. Postmaster General,*[9] the Court considered the constitutionality of a federal law that required pieces of mail judged to be communist political propaganda to be held until the addressee was notified. The addressee must request receipt in writing before it could be delivered. The question the Court asked was whether this represented an unconstitutional abridgment of the addressee's (as opposed to the sender's) First Amendment rights?

The case arose out of the post office's detention in 1963 of the *Peking Review No. 12* addressed to Dr. Corliss Lamont. Instead of responding to the notice of detention, Dr. Lamont instituted a suit to enjoin enforcement of the law: the Postal Service and Federal Employees Salary Act of 1962. The Court concluded that "the Act as construed and applied is unconstitutional because it requires an official act (viz., returning the reply card) as a limitation on the unfettered exercise of the addressee's First Amendment rights."[10]

The Court reasoned that the requirement was almost certain to have a deterrent effect on the First Amendment rights of the addressees. Anyone is likely to feel some inhibition in sending for literature that federal officials have condemned as "communist political propaganda." In the opinion of the Court, "The regime of this Act is therefore at war with the uninhibited, robust, and wide open debate and discussion that are contemplated by the First Amendment."[11]

In a concurring opinion, Justice Brennan pointed out that in this case it is not the sender's right to distribute that is being considered but, rather the addressee's claim. Justice Brennan states that because this case upholds *Martin*(supra), he joins the Court's decision. Government is powerless to interfere with the delivery of this material because the First Amendment necessarily protects the right to receive it. While it is true that the First Amendment contains no specific guarantee of access to publications, the protection of the Bill of Rights goes beyond the specific guarantees to protect from congressional abridgment those equally fundamental personal rights necessary to make the express guarantees fully meaningful.[12] Without the right to receive publications, the right to freedom of speech is meaningless. After all, concludes Justice Brennan: "The dissemination of ideas can accomplish nothing if otherwise willing addressees are not free to receive and consider them. *It would be a barren marketplace of ideas that only had sellers and no buyers.*"[13] [emphasis added].

June 1965

In *Griswold v. Connecticut*[14] the Court followed the precedent set by the two previous cases. Dr. Griswold was executive director of the Planned Parenthood League of Connecticut, and Dr. Buxton served as medical director for the league at its center in New Haven, Connecticut. Both doctors gave information, instruction, and medical advice to married persons concerning means of preventing conception. Such advise was prohibited under Connecticut statutes. The Court ruled the statute unconstitutional on several grounds. Citing *Martin,* the Court stated that "the State may not consistently, with the spirit of the First Amendment, contract the spectrum of available knowledge."[15] Freedom of speech and of the press according to the Court, "includes not only the right to utter or to print, but the right to distribute, the right to receive, the right to read . . . and freedom of inquiry, freedom of thought, and freedom to teach. . . . Without those peripheral rights the specific rights would be less secure."[16]

April 1969

In *Stanley v, Georgia*[17] the Court addressed an important question. If the state can protect the body of a citizen, may it not also protect the mind?

While executing a search warrant for evidence of bookmaking, federal and state agents found and seized three obscene films. Mr. Stanley was then arrested and indicted for the knowing possession of obscene matter in violation of Georgia law. Stanley objected on the ground that the statute was unconstitutional because it punishes mere private possession of obscene matter. Citing *Martin, Griswold,* and *Lamont* (supra), the Court stated: "It is now well established that the Constitution protects the right to receive information and ideas."[18]

The Court reasoned that this right, regardless of the information's social worth, is fundamental to a free society. Along with the right to read or observe what he pleases, there is the right "to satisfy his intellectual and emotional needs in the privacy of his own home."[19] A state may no more prohibit mere possession of obscene material on the ground that it may lead to antisocial conduct than it may prohibit possession of chemistry books on the ground that they may lead to the manufacture of homemade spirits.[20] Neither the states nor Congress can constitutionally premise legislation on the desirability of controlling a person's private thoughts.[21]

To the state's assertion that it has the right to protect an individual's mind from the effects of obscenity, the Court replied: "We are not certain that this argument amounts to anything more than the assertion that the State has the right to control the moral content of a person's thoughts."[22] While this may be a noble purpose, it is wholly inconsistent with the philosophy of the First Amendment in this instance.

1969

In *Red Lion Broadcasting Co. v. Federal Communications Commission*[23] the Court extended the right to receive information to a commercial institution, the broadcasting industry. Under the FCC fairness doctrine, when a personal attack was made in the context of controversial public issues, the broadcast licensee was required to notify the individual or group mentioned and offer a reasonable opportunity to respond over the air. Broadcasters challenged this rule on First Amendment grounds. They argued that the First Amendment protects their desire to use their allocated frequencies in whatever way they chose and to exclude whomever they chose from using their frequencies.

The Court ruled that the federal government may limit the use of broadcast equipment, and that the right of free speech does not embrace a right to snuff out the free speech of others. There is nothing in the First Amendment that prevents the federal government from requiring licensees to share their frequencies with others. "It is the right of viewers and listeners, not the right of the broadcasters, which is paramount."[24]

The purpose of the First Amendment is to preserve an uninhibited marketplace of ideas, not to approve a monopolization of the marketplace. In the opinion of the Court, "It is the right of the public to receive suitable access to social, political, aesthetic, moral, and other ideas and experiences which is crucial here."[25]

1972

In *Kleindienst v. Mandel*[26] the Court set a limit on the right to receive information. This case considered whether the refusal to allow an alien scholar to enter the United States to attend academic meetings violates the First Amendment rights of American scholars and students who wish to hear, speak, and debate with him. The case involved Ernest E. Mandel, a Belgian citizen and editor of the Belgian left socialist weekly, *La Gauche,* who had been invited by the Graduate Student Association at Stanford University to participate in a conference. Mandel had been found ineligible for admission under the Immigration and Nationality Act which barred those who advocated doctrines of world communism.

The Attorney General declined to waive Mandel's ineligibility. Mandel and eight university professors who were United States citizens instituted an action to compel the Attorney General to allow Mandel's admission to the United States so that he could speak at universities and participate in colloquia. They contended that the concern of the First Amendment was not with Mandel's interest in entering and being heard but with the citizens in hearing Mandel explain and defend his views.

Citing *Martin, Lamont, Stanley, Red Lion,* and *Keyishian,* the Court acknowledged that in a variety of contexts, it had recognized a First Amendment right to receive information and ideas.[27] However, the Court also noted that, without exception, they had sustained Congress' power to make rules for the admission of aliens or to prescribe the terms and conditions under which aliens might come to the United States. The Court reasoned that if the First Amendment argument prevailed whenever a bona fide claim was made by American citizens wishing to meet and talk with excluded aliens, Congress's authority would be a nullity, or the Court would be required to weigh the strength of the audience's interest against that of the government in refusing a waiver. The dangers and undesirability of making that determination seem obvious and the Court upheld Congress' authority to exclude Mandel over the constitutional right to receive ideas and information.

1978

In *First National Bank of Boston v. Bellotti*[28] the Court considered whether speech that would otherwise be protected by the First Amendment loses that protection when its source is a corporation. The case involved a challenge to a Massachusetts criminal statute prohibiting banks and business corporations from making contributions or expenditures to influence votes on referendum proposals. The First National Bank of Boston wished to spend money to publicize its views on a proposed constitutional amendment that dealt with a graduated income tax on individuals.

The bank argued that the statute violated the First Amendment. The Court agreed noting that the First Amendment goes beyond the protection of the press and the self-expression of individuals. The First Amendment prohibits government from limiting the stock of information from which members of the public may draw. In the Court's view, "A commercial advertisement is constitutionally protected not so much because it pertains to the seller's business as because it furthers the societal interest in the 'free flow of commercial information.'"[29] Citing *Stanley* and *Red Lion* (supra), the Court concluded that such commercial speech affords the public "access to discussion, debate, and the dissemination of information and ideas"[30] when it deals with public debate over controversial interests. Legislatures are thus disqualified from dictating the subjects and the speakers who may address a public issue.[31] For "[i]f a legislature may direct business corporations to 'stick to business,' it may also limit other corporations—religious, charitable, or civic—to their respective 'business' when addressing the public."[32]

1982

In *Board of Education v. Pico*,[33] (cited hereafter as *Pico*) the Court considered the constitutional right to receive information and ideas as it relates to libraries. The question presented in this case was whether the First Amendment imposes limitations on the exercise by a local school board of its discretion to remove library books from high school and junior high school libraries. In February 1976, the Board of Education of the Island Trees Union Free School District No. 26, in New York, gave an "unofficial direction" that 10 books in the high school library and one book in the junior high school library were to be removed from the library shelves and delivered to the board's office so that board members could read them.

A press release from the board characterized the books as "anti-American, anti-Christian, anti-Sem[i]tic, and just plain filthy."[34] The release concluded: "[I]t is our duty, our moral obligation, to protect the children in our schools from this moral danger as surely as from physical and medical dangers."[35] A short time later, the Board appointed a Book Review Committee to read the books and to recommend to the board whether the books should be retained. In July the committee made its final report, recommending that five of the books be retained and that two others be removed from the school libraries. On the remaining four books the committee was divided. The board subsequently rejected the committee's report and decided that only one book should be returned to the High School Library and that another should be made available subject to parental consent. The Board gave no reason for rejecting the recommendations of the Committee it had appointed.

A group of students brought an action in U. S. District Court, claiming that the Board's action denied them their rights under the First Amendment. The students asked for a declaration that the board's actions were unconstitutional, and for an injunction ordering the board to return the books to the school libraries. The district court substantially agreed with the Board's motivation reasoning that: "The board has restricted access only to certain books which the board believed to be, in essence, vulgar. While removal of such books from a school library may . . . reflect a misguided educational philosophy, it does not constitute a sharp and direct infringement of any first amendment right."[36]

The U. S. Court of Appeals reversed the decision of the U. S. District Court. The U. S. Supreme Court then agreed to hear the case. The Court began by noting that the only books at issue in this case are library books, which are not required as part of the school's curriculum, and that this issue does not involve the acquisition of new books for the library. The students were not trying to compel the board to add to the school library shelves any books that students desire to read. The only action being challenged was the removal from the school libraries of books originally placed there by the school authorities, or at least without objections from them.[37]

While acknowledging that the Court had long recognized that local school boards have broad discretion in the management of school affairs, it held that the discretion of these local and state boards must comport with the "transcendent imperatives of the First Amendment."[38] Boards of education are educating the young for citizenship. If the boards do not scrupulously protect the constitutional freedoms of the individuals they "strangle the free mind at its source and teach youth to discount important principles of our government as mere platitudes."[39] First Amendment rights are thus available to students.

The Court noted that courts in general should not intervene in the daily operation of school systems unless basic constitutional values are directly and sharply implicated. In this case, because of the right of students to receive information and ideas, the Court must intervene. In the opinion of the Court, the First Amendment rights of students are directly and sharply implicated by the removal of books from the shelves of a school library.

Citing *First National Bank, Griswold, Stanley, Struthers*, and *Lamont* (supra), the Court reasoned that the First Amendment affords the public access to discussion, debate, and the dissemination of information and ideas. The right to receive information and ideas is an inherent corollary of the rights of free speech and press in two senses. First, the right to receive ideas follows ineluctably from the *sender's* First Amendment right to send them. In Martin it was stated that the right of freedom of speech and of the press protects the right to receive it. The dissemination of ideas cannot accomplish anything if willing addressees are not free to receive and consider them. As Justice Brennan stated in *Lamont*(supra): [I]t would be a barren marketplace of ideas that had only sellers and no buyers; but more importantly, "the right to receive ideas is a necessary predicate to the *recipient's* meaningful exercise of his own rights of speech, press, and political freedom."[40]

In short, just as access to ideas makes it possible for citizens to exercise their rights of free speech and press in a meaningful manner, such access prepares students for active and effective participation in the pluralistic, often contentious society in which they will soon be adult members. Of course, the First Amendment rights of students must be viewed in the school environment. The Court noted:

But the special characteristics of the school *library* make that environment especially appropriate for the recognition of the First Amendment rights of students.A school library, no less than any other public library, is "a place dedicated to quiet, to knowledge, and to beauty." *Brown v. Louisiana*, 383 U. S. 131, 142(1966)(opinion of Fortas, J.). *Keyishian v. Board of Regents*, 385 U. S. 589(1967), observed that "students must always remain free to inquire, to study and to evaluate, to gain new maturity and understanding." The school library is the principal locus of such freedom.[41]

Quoting a district court opinion, the Court notes that in a school library "a student can literally explore the unknown, and discover areas of interest and thought not covered by the prescribed curriculum. . . . Th[e] student learns that a library is a place to test or expand upon ideas presented to him, in or out of the classroom." The school board emphasized that it must be allowed *unfettered* discretion to transmit community values. This claim, according to the court, overlooks the unique role of the school library: "It appears from the record that the use of the Island Trees school libraries is completely voluntary on the part of students. Their selection of books from these libraries is entirely a matter of free choice; the libraries afford them an opportunity at self-education and individual enrichment that is wholly optional."[42]

The board's reliance on its claim of absolute discretion beyond the compulsory environment of the classroom is misplaced in "the school library and the regime of voluntary inquiry that there holds sway."[43]

To what extent then does the First Amendment place limitations on the board's discretion to remove books from school libraries? The Court noted that while the board has significant discretion in determining the content of school libraries, that discretion may not be exercised in a narrowly political manner: "If a Democratic school board, motivated by party affiliation, ordered the removal of all books written by or in favor of Republicans, few would doubt that the order violated the constitutional rights of the students denied access to those books;"[44] The Constitution "does not permit the official suppression of *ideas*."[45] If the Board *intended* to deny students' access to ideas with which it disagreed, and that was a decisive factor in its decision, then the board exercised its discretion in violation of the Constitution. If the decision to remove the books was based solely on their educational suitability, the removal would be permissible.

The Court then looked at the particulars of this case to determine if there was evidence of the motivation behind the board's removal decision. The Court noted that there was no record of an established, regular, and facially unbiased procedure for review of controversial materials. In fact quite the opposite was true. The board had indeed ignored the views of librarians and teachers, the superintendent of schools and the "guidance of publications that rate books for junior and senior high school students."[46] Based on the evidence, the board's removal decision seemed highly irregular and ad hoc. The court ordered the case back to the lower courts to determine the Board's actual motivation.

There were four dissenting decisions in this case. While none contested the right to receive information, the dissenters argued that the students could not freely exercise this right in the public school setting. Justice Rehnquist noted that the libraries of elementary and secondary schools serve a different purpose than other libraries: "Unlike universities or public libraries, elementary and secondary schools are not designed for freewheeling inquiry; they are tailored, to teaching of basic skills and ideas."[47]

LIBRARIES AND THE RIGHT TO INFORMATION

Access to Libraries

In 1992 the United States Court of Appeals for the Third Circuit considered the constitutional right of access to information and ideas in relation to the public's right of access to libraries. The case concerned a public library's authority to promulgate and enforce regulations governing the use of their facilities. A homeless man, Richard R. Kreimer, was expelled from the Joint Free Public Library of Morristown and Morris Township for violating rules governing patron conduct. Kreimer filed suit in the U. S. District Court of New Jersey alleging that the library rules were facially invalid under the First and Fourteenth Amendment. The District Court accepted Kreimer's arguments and issued an interlocutory injunction prohibiting enforcement of several of the library's rules.

Kreimer based his First Amendment claim on the constitutional right to receive information and ideas. In his brief, he cited the "vital role played by public libraries" in promoting the fullest exercise of that right. After reviewing *Martin, Lamont, Griswold, Stanley, Red Lion Broadcasting,* and *Pico,* the Court of Appeals agreed that the constitutional right to receive information was implicated in this case, and there was thus a right to "some level of access to a public library" in the First Amendment. Like other First Amendment rights, however, the right to receive information is not "unfettered and may give way to significant countervailing interests."[48] For one, there are reasonable time, manner, and place restrictions.

In this case, the circuit court found that the library's rules were reasonable "manner" restrictions on Kreimer's constitutional right to receive information.[49] The library's interest in achieving the optimum and best use of its facilities warranted restricting Kreimer's access to the library. Libraries are in general places dedicated to quiet, knowledge, and to beauty.[50] This Library was established as a place to aid acquisition of knowledge through reading, writing, and quiet contemplation. The exercise of other more verbal interactive First Amendment activities was ruled to be antithetical to the nature of the library.[51]

In short, the circuit court held in this case that a library is a public forum, but it is a limited public forum. It is limited to those activities that are consistent with the nature of a library as a place of study. These types of activities are protected by the First Amendment, but the library may legitimately regulate other activities.

Library Records

The U.S. Supreme Court has not yet ruled on the constitutional right of access to libraries expounded in *Kreimer*. Neither has it considered the issue of the confidentiality of records resulting from the exercise of that right, or whether making those records accessible to the public would impair the exercise of that right of access. The Court has, however, ruled in *Pico* that the First Amendment right to receive information and ideas—the root of the public's right of access to its libraries—must give way to a significant countervailing public interest.

FOIA

That countervailing public interest is the Freedom of Information Act(FOIA) which guarantees citizens the general right of access to government records (see Appendix B). The earliest FOIA predecessor was the 1789 housekeeping statute, which gave federal agencies the authority to regulate their business, set up filing systems, and keep records. This law gave executive agencies the authority to withold information and control the availability of records to the public when

it saw fit. In 1958 Congress amended this law reducing that authority. Only after eight years of extensive investigative and legislative
hearings did Congress do away with that discretionary authority. On
July 4, 1967, FOIA became effective and, thereafter, completely
changed the presumptions about the accessibility of government
records.

Prior to the enactment of FOIA, the burden was on the individual
to establish a right to examine government records. There were no
statutory guidelines or procedures to help someone seeking records,
and there were no remedies if he or she were denied access. Following
the passage of FOIA the old presumption was completely replaced
with a new one—government records in the possession of agencies
and departments of the executive branch are to be accessible to
citizens. The burden of proof shifted from the individual to the
government. The need to know requirement was replaced by the right
to know doctrine. Government now had to justify the need for secrecy
and for denying access to records. Under FOIA, federal agencies are
required to provide the fullest possible disclosure of information to
the public.[52]

The basic purpose behind FOIA is to ensure that an informed
citizenry will hold government accountable to the governed and act as
a check against corruption.[53] Thus FOIA guarantees the right of
citizens to know about the business of their government.[54] Under
FOIA, an agency may only withhold a document if the information in
it falls within one of nine statutory exemptions, and invoking those
exemptions is in most cases optional. Agency decisions to withhold
records or other information may also be challenged in federal court,
and in such cases the burden of proof for withholding is on the agency,
not the individual bringing suit.

The general policy of FOIA favoring public access is grounded in
the constitutional right to receive and gain access to information and
ideas. Its purpose of providing access to government information so
that citizens can find out what their government is up to is at the
heart of the First Amendment. Thus to deny or interfere arbitrarily
with access to this important government information is an abridgement of the freedoms of speech and of the press protected by the First
Amendment.[55]

While FOIA is limited to federal agencies, many states have
followed the federal example and passed their legislation modeled on
the federal law. The enactment of these FOIA statutes without a
specific exemption for library records, provides the basis for requests
by law enforcement agencies to see these records as part of their

investigations. Once these records became available to the general public, these agencies reasoned that they were available for criminal or national security investigations as well.

The complete story has not yet been told. FOIA has exemptions and is subject to another penumbral right—the constitutional right to privacy.

Notes

1. *Kreimer v. Bureau of Police for Town of Morristown*, 958 F.2d 1242 at 1255 (1992).
2. 319 U.S. 141
3. Ibid. at 143.
4. Ibid.
5. Ibid. at 145. "While door to door distributors of literature may be either a nuisance or a blind for criminal activities, they may also be useful members of society engaged in the dissemination of ideas in accordance with the best tradition of free discussion."
6. Ibid. at 146-147.
7. Ibid.
8. Ibid.
9. 381 U.S. 301.
10. Ibid. at 305.
11. Ibid. at 307.
12. Ibid. at 308.
13. Ibid.
14. 381 U.S. 479.
15. Ibid. at 482-483.
16. Ibid.
17. 394 U.S. 557.
18. Ibid. at 564.
19. Ibid. at 565.
20. Ibid. at 567.
21. Ibid. at 566.
22. Ibid. at 565.
23. 395 U.S. 369.
24. Ibid. at 390.
25. Ibid.
26. 408 U.S. 753.
27. Ibid. at 762.
28. 435 U.S. 765.
29. Ibid. at 783.
30. Ibid.
31. Ibid. at 786.
32. Ibid. at 785.
33. 457 U.S. 853.

34. Ibid. at 857.
35. 474 F.Supp. 387 at 390(1979).
36. Ibid. at 397.
37. *Pico* at 862.
38. Ibid. at 864.
39. *West Virginia Board of Education v. Barnette*, 319 U.S. 624 at 637(1943).
40. Ibid. at 867.
41. Ibid. at 868-869.
42. *Pico* at 869.
43. Ibid.
44. Ibid. at 871.
45. Ibid.
46. Ibid. at 874.
47. Ibid. at 915.
48. Ibid.
49. Ibid. at 1246.
50. *Brown v. Louisiana*, 383 U.S. 131 at 142(1966).
51. *Kreimer* at 1261.
52. House Report 100-199, Committee on Government Operations. 100th Congress 1st session.
53. *NLRB v. Robbins Tire & Rubber Co.*, 437 U.S. 214 at 242(1978).
54. House Report(Government Operations Committee) No. 93-876, March 5, 1974 [To accompany H.R. 12471], p.3.
55. *Richmond Newspapers, Inc., v. Virginia*, 448 U.S. 555 at 583(1980).

3
Constitutional Right to Privacy

- *What is the relationship between the First Amendment and the constitutional right to privacy?*
- *Under what provisions of the Constitution is the right to privacy guaranteed?*
- *Does this constitutional right to privacy protect the confidentiality of library records?*

Privacy is among the rights most cherished by Americans. In 1928 Justice Brandeis called it "the most comprehensive of rights and the right most valued by civilized men."[1] Today public opinion polls indicate that Americans treasure privacy as much in the abstract as they do in their daily lives.[2]

The Constitution does not explicitly establish a right of privacy. The Court, however, in interpreting that Constitution, has recognized for over 100 years that a right of personal privacy exists.[3] In this chapter the constitutional right of privacy is carefully examined to determine what protection it offers to the confidentiality of library records. We begin by analyzing the Court's recognition of the constitutional right to privacy. The role of that right in the disclosure of personal records held by government is then considered.

Definition

Privacy is a broad, abstract and somewhat ambiguous concept,[4] for which the Court has not yet delineated any comprehensive definition. In 1928 Justice Brandeis referred to privacy as simply the "right to be let alone,"[5] and almost 40 years later the same words were still being used by the Court.[6] Since the Constitution only defines the rights of citizens as they relate to government(not as they relate to each other), privacy in this sense means the right to be free of unjustifiable intrusion by government upon the individual. The Court has seen this as involving two distinct interests: 1) the individual's interest in avoiding disclosure of personal matters by the government, which we will call *disclosural* privacy;[7] and 2) the interest in independence from government in making certain decisions in such personal areas as family, travel and education,[8] which we will call *autonomy*.[9]

Like other Constitutional rights, the right to privacy is part of the concept of liberty and the pursuit of happiness described in the *Declaration of Independence* as an inalienable right.[10] It is a fundamental right[11] that is deep-rooted in our society;[12] the Court has speculated that it existed long before the Bill of Rights.[13]

Source

The word *privacy* is not used in the Constitution or Bill of Rights, and the right of privacy cannot be inferred from any single amendment. One member of the Court, Justice Black, doubted that a general right to privacy could be found in the Constitution.[14] On the other hand, Justice Douglas felt that it emanated from the totality of the constitutional scheme.[15] The roots of the right to privacy have generally been traced by the Court to the guarantees of rights in several amendments and in their penumbras. These guarantees create constitutional zones of privacy into which government may not intrude.

First Amendment

One of these roots is the First Amendment. As we have seen in chapter 1, the First Amendment has penumbral rights which, while not specifically mentioned in its clauses, are essential to the full exercise of the rights that are specifically enumerated in the amendment. The Court has acknowledged that the First Amendment includes the penumbral right to: educate a child in a school of their parents' choice;[16] study any particular subject or any foreign language;[17] read;[18] inquire, think, or teach;[19] and receive information and ideas (see chapter 2).

The First Amendment right to freedom of association can also be found in the amendment's periphery or penumbra.

The right of association was first enunciated by the Court in 1958. In that case, which involved the National Association for the Advancement of Colored People (NAACP), the Court reasoned that the full exercise of freedom of speech includes the freedom to engage in association for the advancement of beliefs and ideas.[20] If an association like NAACP were required by law to reveal the names and addresses of its membership, that compelled disclosure could result in a substantial restraint on the members' personal freedom to associate. In the case of groups with dissident views, such disclosure might expose its members to threats, loss of employment, and public hostility. It might result in members withdrawing from the association and dissuading others from joining it because of fear of exposure of their beliefs.[21] In short, the First Amendment must protect the association members' privacy from government intrusion if the rights explicitly guaranteed in the First Amendment are to have any utility at all.

The Court has held that this right of privacy in association applies to political, social, and legal associations as well as associations formed for the economic benefit of the members.[22] The right also goes beyond limiting disclosure of membership lists. In 1957 the Court held that it is not permissible to bar a lawyer from practicing law because he had once been a member of the Communist Party.[23] Membership in a group must go beyond the right to attend a meeting. It must also include the right to express one's attitudes or philosophies by membership in a group or by affiliation with it. Association is a form of expression of opinion, and while it is not expressly included in the First Amendment, its existence is necessary to make its express guarantees fully meaningful.[24] The Court has noted that "the First Amendment has a penumbra where privacy is protected from governmental intrusion,"[25] and this is a constitutional zone of privacy.

Third Amendment

Another root of the constitutional right of privacy is the Third Amendment. Its prohibition against the quartering of soldiers "in any house" in time of peace without the consent of the owner is another aspect of freedom from government intrusion.[26] It is the right of civilians to be left alone in their own homes, at least in times of peace. The Third Amendment creates a constitutional zone of privacy in this instance.

Fourth Amendment

This ammendment explicitly affirms that the "right of the people to be secure in their persons, houses, papers, and effects, against unreasonable searches and seizures shall not be violated. . . ."[27] The

Fourth Amendment is rooted in a 1765 English case,[28] which determined that British law did not allow officers of the Crown to break into a citizen's home, under cover of a general assistance writ, to search for evidence of the utterance of libel.[29] English authorities used these writs in colonial times to enter any house to seize smuggled goods.

In 1961 the Court referred to the Fourth Amendment as creating a "right to privacy, no less important than any other right carefully and particularly reserved to the people."[30] In 1965 the Court interpreted this amendment as creating a constitutional zone of privacy.[31] In 1967 the Court held that the Fourth Amendment protects people, not places: "What a person knowingly exposes to the public, even in his own home or office, is not a subject of Fourth Amendment protection. . . . But what he seeks to preserve as private, even in an area accessible to the public, may be constitutionally protected."[32] This is the source of the Court's current practice of inquiring in criminal search and seizure cases as to whether the defendant had a "reasonable expectation of privacy" in the area where evidence was found by the police.

Fifth Amendment

The Self-Incrimination Clause[33] of the Fifth Amendment also creates a zone of privacy.[34] Government may not force persons to act as witness against themselves, surrendering this zone of privacy to their detriment. The Self-Incrimination Clause was intended to prevent the use of the English ex officio oaths. These oaths required defendants to admit their crimes. During the period of the infamous Star Chamber in England, these oaths were used to root out political heresies.

In an 1886 case, the Court described the Fourth and Fifth Amendments as protection against all governmental invasions of the "sanctity of a man's home and the privacies of life."[35] In 1966 the Court stated that the Fifth Amendment reflects the Constitution's concern for the right of each individual "to a private enclave where he may lead a private life."[36]

Ninth Amendment

Unlike the other original amendments in the Bill of Rights, the Ninth Amendment does not enumerate any specific rights. Instead it opens the door to other rights not specifically mentioned in the first eight amendments. In a concurring opinion in a 1965 case, Justice

Goldberg reasoned that both the language and the history of the Ninth Amendment indicate that the framers of the Constitution believed that there are additional fundamental rights that exist alongside the rights mentioned in the first eight amendments.

The Ninth Amendment states: "The enumeration in the Constitution, of certain rights, shall not be construed to deny or disparage others retained by the people." The Ninth Amendment was introduced by James Madison in order to quiet fears that a bill of specifically enumerated rights would not be broad enough to cover all essential rights. It was feared that the specific mention of a right would be interpreted as a denial that others are protected.[37]

Justice Goldberg argues that this makes it clear that the first eight amendments were not intended to be construed to exhaust the basic and fundamental rights that the Constitution guaranteed. He states: "To hold that a right so basic and fundamental and so deeply rooted in our society as the right of privacy in marriage may be infringed because that right is not guaranteed in so many words by the first eight amendments to the Constitution is to ignore the Ninth Amendment and to give it no effect whatsoever."[38]

Fourteenth Amendment

Another root of the constitutional right of privacy is the concept of liberty as it is used in the Fourteenth Amendment. The first paragraph of the Fourteenth Amendment includes the phrase, "nor shall any state deprive any person of life, *liberty*, or property, without due process of law. . ." (emphasis added).[39] While the Court has not attempted to specifically define the concept of liberty as it is used in this phrase, it has enumerated several rights that are guaranteed by the concept of liberty.

In a 1923 ruling, the Court stated that:

> Without doubt, it [liberty] denotes not merely freedom from bodily restraint, but also the right of the individual to contract, to engage in any of the common occupations of life, *to acquire useful knowledge*, to marry, establish a home and bring up children, to worship God according to the dictates of his own conscience, and, generally, to enjoy those privileges long recognized at common law as essential to the orderly pursuit of happiness by free men [40] [emphasis added].

The Fourteenth Amendment protects these and other rights that are so rooted in the traditions and conscience of the American people as to be considered *fundamental*. For example, freedom of thought and speech is a fundamental right because it is the indispensable condition of nearly every form of freedom. With rare exception, that recognition can be found throughout America's history, both political and legal. It is also a logical imperative when it is realized that liberty is more than exemption from physical restraint. Liberty would not exist if that right was sacrificed.[41] States cannot deprive any person of these liberties arbitrarily or without a reasonable relation to that state's interest—in other words "without due process," as is stated in the first paragraph of the Fourteenth Amendment.

Nature of the right

The right to privacy, which gets its life and substance from these various amendments, is not, however, absolute. Like the amendments from which it is derived, the constitutional right to privacy has limitations and exceptions. These limitations and exceptions can be seen when the constitutional right to privacy is applied to records kept by government.

GOVERNMENT RECORDS AND THE RIGHT TO PRIVACY

While virtually every government action interferes in some way with personal privacy, the question the courts must ask is whether that government interference violates a right guaranteed by the Constitution.[42] Appendix C presents excerpts from Supreme Court opinions on the right of privacy. Most of the privacy cases decided by the Court have been concerned with autonomy. This type of case involves government interference in an individual's decisions within the zones of privacy. The Court has, however, said little about the constitutional dimensions of disclosural privacy. There are three notable exceptions.

Marital relationship

In 1965 the Court decided the case of *Griswold v. Connecticut*.[43] Both Dr. Griswold and Dr. Buxton ran the Planned Parenthood League of Connecticut. Dr. Griswold was the executive director and Dr. Buxton, medical director of its center in New Haven. As part of their duties, both doctors provided information, instruction, and medical advice to married persons concerning means of preventing conception. Following a medical examination, they prescribed the best contraceptive device or material for use. Under Connecticut statute at the time, it was illegal to use contraceptive devices or to assist, abet, or counsel another in their use. Both doctors were found guilty as accessories.

The Court ruled the statute unconstitutional on several grounds. One was that the marital relationship lies within the zone of privacy. The Court reasoned that the law forbidding the use of contraceptives attempts to accomplish its goal by means that have the maximum destructive impact on the marital relationship. The law could have just as easily regulated the manufacture or sale of contraceptive devices. Instead it used means that were unnecessarily broad. The Court asked: "Would we allow the police to search the sacred precincts of marital bedrooms for telltale signs of the use of contraceptives?"[44] Such an idea, it stated, is "repulsive to the notions of privacy surrounding the marriage relationship."[45] The Court noted: "We deal with a right of privacy older than the Bill of Rights—older than our political parties, older than our school system. Marriage is a coming together for better or for worse, hopefully enduring, and intimate to the degree of being sacred."[46]

The Connecticut statute was ruled unconstitutional because it would require government to acquire information about individuals' activities within one of their zones of privacy, the marital relationship. Government, despite its enormous investigative powers, must not intrude upon these areas.

Computerized records

In 1977 in *Whalen v. Roe*[47] the Court considered the constitutionality of a New York statute that required recording in a centralized computer file the names and addresses of all persons who had obtained a doctor's prescription for certain drugs. The drugs included, but were not limited to, those that have an illegal market. A lower court had ruled that creating such a computer file invaded a constitutionally protected zone of privacy, the doctor/patient relationship, and that the act invaded this relationship with "a needlessly broad sweep."[48] The lower court also felt that New York State had not demonstrated the necessity for maintaining such a file.

Appellants argued that the file created a genuine concern that the information would become publicly known and would adversely affect their reputations. Such possible disclosure would make some patients reluctant to use, and some doctors reluctant to prescribe, drugs that are medically indicated. The Court, however, did not feel that the program posed a sufficiently grievous threat to the reputation or independence of patients.

The Court reasoned that there were three ways in which the public disclosure could occur: health department employees might violate the statute by failing, either deliberately or negligently, to maintain proper security; a patient or doctor might be accused of a violation and the file would then be offered as evidence in a judicial proceeding; and a doctor, pharmacist, or patient might reveal information on a prescription form. The Court considered each in turn. It found nothing in the experience of other states who have had similar programs to indicate that the security provisions of the program would be administered improperly. The Court also did not believe that the remote possibility of public disclosure as a result of judicial proceeding offered a sufficient reason for invalidating the entire patient-identification program. Many states recognize the physician/patient privilege, which precludes certain records from being admitted into evidence. The Court considered the third argument—the risk of a breech in security—as being unrelated to the computerization of the file.

Concerning the issue of patients and doctors being reluctant to use or prescribe drugs, the Court responded that there are a "host of other unpleasant invasions of privacy that are associated with many facets of health care."[49] The Court observed that it is an essential part of medical practices today to require patients to disclose private medical information to doctors, hospital personnel, insurance companies, and public health agencies, even when such disclosures may reflect unfavorably on their character. While the record indicates that some use of drugs has been discouraged because information about who is using them is readily available in a computer file, the record also indicates that 100,000 prescriptions are continuing to be filled each month.

The Court also pointed out that no individual has been deprived of the right to decide independently, with the advice of his or her doctor, to acquire or to use needed medication. New York State has not totally prohibited the use of particular drugs nor does the state require the consent of any official or third party to prescribe the drugs. The decision to use or prescribe is left entirely to the physician and the patient.

The Court also considered the significant state interest involved. New York State has a strong interest in preventing drugs from being diverted into unlawful channels. To answer the lower court's contention that New York State was unable to demonstrate the necessity for such a computer file system, the Court replied: "State legislation which has some effect on individual liberty or privacy may not be held unconstitutional simply because a court finds it unnecessary, in whole or in part. For we have frequently recognized that individual States have broad latitude in experimenting with possible solutions to problems of vital local concern."[50]

For these reasons the Court ruled that the New York statute does not invade the constitutional right to privacy.

Presidential records

In 1977, in the case of *Nixon v. Administrator of General Services*,[51] the Court considered the constitutionality of the Presidential Recordings and Materials Preservation Act as it related to the 42 million pages of documents and 880 tape recordings of former President Nixon. After resigning from office, President Richard Nixon executed a depository agreement with the General Services Administrator (GSA). The agreement called for the records and recordings to be stored near the Nixons' California home. Neither the former President nor the GSA could gain access to the material without the other's consent. The agreement also called for the eventual destruction of the tapes. After a five-year period, GSA would destroy all of the tapes the former President directed, and after ten years the rest would be destroyed.

After the terms of the agreement were made public, a bill was introduced in Congress and three months later it was passed and then signed into law by President Ford. The act directed GSA to take custody of the former president's materials and have them screened by government archivists to determine which were private in nature and which had historical value. President Nixon immediately started a court action challenging the constitutionality of the act, in part on the grounds that it violated his privacy interests in avoiding disclosure of personal matters.

The Court acknowledged that public officials, including the President, have constitutionally protected privacy rights in that part of their personal life that is unrelated to any acts performed in their public capacity. The former President had a reasonable expectation of privacy in withholding matters concerning his family or personal finances. Against the merits of President Nixon's claim of invasion of privacy, however, must be weighed the public's interest in subjecting the presidential materials to archival screening. In this instance, the Court found the former President's interest to be weaker than that of the appellants in *Whalen*.

The Court found that the intrusion in this case is very limited. The act mandates promulgation of regulations aimed at preventing undue dissemination of private materials. The purely private papers were to be returned to the former President. The overwhelming bulk of the material relates to the official conduct of the Presidency. Some documents and tapes had already been disclosed to the public. In short, the privacy claim relates to only a very small fraction of the massive volume of official materials. The court concluded that the act is the least intrusive manner in which to provide an adequate level of promotion of government interests of overriding importance.

Records kept by government

Whalen and *Nixon* indicate some important points about the relationship between records and the constitutional right to privacy. First, the government's right to reveal information about an individual conflicts with the individual's constitutional right of privacy when the government's action restricts the individual's freedom in the zone of privacy.[52] As we have seen, the Court has so far explicitly enumerated these zones of privacy as including activities relating to marriage, procreation, contraception, family relationships, or child rearing and education.[53] The right of association has also been explicitedly placed within this zone of privacy.[54] In 1992 the Court said: "[T]hese matters, involving the most intimate and personal choices a person may make in a lifetime, [are] choices central to personal dignity and autonomy."[55] These decisions are central to liberty because, in the words of the Court, they "define one's own concept of existence, of meaning, of the universe, and of the mystery of human life."[56] Beliefs about these matters would not define personhood if they were formed under the compulsion of government.[57]

Second, persons do not lose their constitutional right to privacy because the records are being kept or held by a government agency. The protection of zones of privacy must include the right to prevent the disclosure of information held by government. This is so even if the information is collected pursuant to a valid governmental objective.[58]

Third, the right to privacy is not absolute. Exceptions are made to information that violates the zones of privacy when the government's interest in disclosure outweighs the individual's privacy interests. In *Whalen* it was noted that a statute that results in a serious deprivation of privacy is still consistent with the Constitution if it promotes a compelling state interest.[59] The courts thus apply a balancing approach to questions of disclosural privacy, weighing each competing interest against the other.

Library records

Libraries are used by people to make the kind of personal and intimate decisions that fall within the constitutional zone of privacy. It is also clear that library patrons take it for granted that these records will not be available for public scrutiny; otherwise they might avoid exploring certain information and ideas and making their own decisions about their value. If library patrons have a privacy interest in these records, the courts will weigh this interest against the public's interest in knowing about these records.

In 1989, the Court considered whether disclosing the contents of FBI criminal identification files, known as rap sheets, to a third party constituted an unwarranted invasion of personal privacy. FOIA makes provisions for safeguarding the personal privacy of individuals. Under Exemption 7(C)[60] records that "could reasonably be expected to constitute an unwarranted invasion of personal privacy" are exempt from disclosure. The Court stated that whether disclosure of a private document is warranted under this exemption turns on the nature of the requested document and its relationship to the basic purpose of FOIA.[61] It does not depend on the particular purpose for which the document is being requested nor does it depend on who is requesting it.

The Court determined that the purpose of FOIA is to guarantee citizens the right to be informed about what their government is up to: "Official information that sheds light on an agency's performance of its statutory duties falls squarely within that statutory purpose."[62] The Court concluded: "That purpose, however, is not fostered by disclosure of information about private citizens that is accumulated in various governmental files but that reveals little or nothing about an agency's own conduct." In these cases, the requester is not trying to discover anything about the conduct of the agency that has possession of the records. "The Court noted that response to this request would not shed any light on the conduct of any Government agency or official."[63] In this case the Court found the public interest in rap sheets falls outside the public interest FOIA was enacted to serve.[64]

Do library records about individual patrons fall outside the public's interest? Do the records kept on individuals reveal anything about what the government is up to? These questions have not been directly addressed by the Court.

In chapter 4, we will determine if the confidentiality of library records is protected by any federal statutes.

Notes

1. *Olmstead v. United States*, 277 U.S. 438 at 478(1928).
2. David F. Linowes, Chairman, *Personal Privacy in an Information Society: The Report of the Privacy Protection Commission*, Washington, D.C.:1977, p.5.
3. *Roe v. Wade*, 410 U.S. 113 at 152 (1973).
4. Dissenting opinion of Justice Black in *Griswold v. Connecticut*, 381 U.S. 479 at 509(1965).
5. Dissenting opinion in *Olmstead* at 478(1928).
6. Majority opinion in *Katz v. United States*, 389 U.S. 347 at 350-351(1967).
7. *Industrial Foundation of the South v. Texas Industrial Accident Board*, 540 S.W.2d 668 at 679(1976), certiorari denied 430 U.S. 931.
8. *Whalen v. Roe*, 429 U.S. 589 at 599-600(1975).
9. *Industrial Foundation of the South* at 679.
10. As stated by Justice Brandeis in *Olmstead*, p. 478: "The makers of our Constitution undertook to secure conditions favorable to the pursuit of happiness. They recognized the significance of man's spiritual nature, of his feelings, and of his intellect. They knew that only a part of the pain, pleasure and satisfactions of life are to be found in material things. They sought to protect Americans in their beliefs, their thoughts, their emotions and their sensations. They conferred as against the Government, the right to be let alone—the most comprehensive of rights and the right most valued by civilized men. To protect that right, every unjustifiable intrusion by the Government upon the privacy of the individual, whatever the means employed, must be deemed a violation. . . ."
11. *Stanley v. Georgia*, 394 U.S. 557 at 564(1969).
12. *Griswold*, p. 491.
13. *Griswold* at 486.
14. In his dissenting opinion to *Griswold* at 508, Justice Black said: "The Court talks about a constitutional 'right of privacy' as though there is some constitutional provision or provisions forbidding any law ever to be passed which might abridge the 'privacy' of individuals. But there is not. There are, of course, guarantees in certain specific constitutional provisions which are designed in part to protect privacy at certain times and places with respect to certain activities."
15. Justice Douglas' dissent in *Poe v. Ullman*, 367 U.S. 497 at 521(1961).
16. *Pierce v. Society of Sisters*, 268 U.S. 33(1925).
17. *Meyer v. Nebraska*, 262 U.S. 390(1923).
18. *Martin v. Struthers*, 319 U.S. 141 at 143(1943).
19. *Wieman v. Updegraff*, 344 U.S. 183 at 195(1952).
20. *NAACP v. Alabama*, 357 U.S. 449 at 460(1958).

21. Ibid. at 463.
22. *NAACP v. Button*, 371 U.S. 415 at 430-431(1963).
23. *Schware v. Board of Bar Examiners*, 353 U.S. 233 at 244(1957).
24. *Griswold* at 483.
25. *Griswold* at 483.
26. The Third Amendment in part states that "No soldier shall, in time of peace be quartered in any house, without the consent of the Owner, nor in time of war, but in a manner to be prescribed by law."
27. The Fourth Amendment states that "The right of the people to be secure in their persons, houses, papers, and effects, against unreasonable searches and seizures, shall not be violated, and no warrants shall issue, but upon probable cause, supported by oath or affirmation, and particularly describing the place to be searched, and the persons or things to be seized."
28. *Entick v. Carrington*, 19 Howell's State Trials, col. 1029.
29. *Frank v. Maryland*, 359 U.S. 360 at 363(1959).
30. *Mapp v. Ohio*, 367 U.S. 643 at 656(1961).
31. *Griswold* at 484.
32. *Katz v. United States*, 389 U.S. 347 at 351(1967).
33. The Fifth Amendment states: "No person shall be held to answer for a capital, or otherwise infamous crime, unless on a presentment or indictment of a Grand Jury, except in cases arising in the land or naval forces, or in the militia, when in actual service in time or war or public danger; nor shall any person be subject for the same offense to be twice put in jeopardy of life or limb; nor shall be compelled in any criminal case to be a witness against himself, nor be deprived or life, liberty, or property, without due process of law; nor shall private property be taken for public use without just compensation." The Self-Incrimination Clause states: ". . . nor shall be compelled in any criminal case to be a witness against himself. . . ."
34. *Griswold* at 484.
35. *Boyd v. United States*, 116 U,S, 616 at 630(1886).
36. *Tehan v. U.S.*, 382 U.S. 406 at 416(1966).
37. *Griswold* at 488-489.
38. *Griswold* at 491.
39. The first clause of the Fourteenth Amendment states: "1. All persons born or naturalized in the United States, and subject to the jurisdiction thereof, are citizens of the United States and of the State wherein they reside. No State shall make or enforce any law which shall abridge the privileges, or immunities of citizens of the United States; nor shall any state deprive any person of life, liberty, or property, without due process of law; nor deny to any person within its jurisdiction the equal protection of the laws."
40. *Meyer* at 399(1923).
41. *Palko v. Connecticut*, 302 U.S. 319 at 325(1937). Rights which are "fundamental" or "implicit in the concept of ordered liberty" are explicated.

42. *Katz* at 350 fn.5.
43. 381 U.S. 479(1965).
44. Ibid. at 485.
45. Ibid. at 485-486.
46. Ibid. at 486.
47. 429 U.S. 589.
48. Ibid. at 596.
49. Ibid. at 602.
50. Ibid. at 597.
51. 433 U.S. 425.
52. *Industrial Foundation of the South* at 680-681.
53. Roe at 152-153.
54. *Griswold* at 484.
55. *Planned Parenthood of Southeastern Pennsylvania v. Casey*, No. 91-744, Slip op. U.S. Supreme Court(June 29, 1992). "Our law affords constitutional protection to personal decisions relating to marriage, procreation, contraception, family relationships, child rearing, and education. *Carey v. Population Services International*, 431 U. S., at 685. Our cases recognize the right of the individual, married or single, to be free from unwarranted governmental intrusion into matters so fundamentally affecting a person as the decision whether to bear or beget a child. *Eisenstadt v. Baird.* . . . Our precedents have respected the private realm of family life which the state cannot enter. *Prince v. Massachusetts*, 321 U.S. 158, 166 (1944). These matters, involving the most intimate and personal choices a person may make in a lifetime, choices central to personal dignity and autonomy, are central to the liberty protected by the Fourteenth Amendment. At the heart of liberty is the right to define one's own concept of existence, of meaning, of the universe, and of the mystery of human life. Beliefs about these matters could not define the attributes of personhood were they formed under compulsion of the State."
56. Ibid.
57. Ibid.
58. In *Industrial Foundation of the South* at 679 the Supreme Court of Texas stated: "The individual does not forfeit all rights to control access to intimate facts concerning his personal life merely because the State has a legitimate interest in obtaining that information."
59. In *Whalen* at 606-607(1977), Justice Brennan in a concurring opinion said: "a statute that did effect such a [serious] deprivation [of privacy] would only be consistent with the Constitution if it were necessary to promote a compelling state interest."
60. Section 552(b)(7)(C). See Appendix B.
61. *United States Department of Justice v. Reporters Committee for Freedom of the Press*, 489 U.S. 749 at 753(1989).
62. Ibid. at 773.
63. Ibid.
64. Ibid. at 775.

4

Federal Laws and Library Records

- *Are there any federal laws which protect the privacy of government records containing information about individuals?*
- *Is there a national law protecting the confidentiality of library records?*
- *How do these privacy laws relate to the Supreme Court's development of the constitutional right to privacy?*

Americans treasure their right to privacy and demand that government not abridge or violate this constitutionally guaranteed right. The enormous information-gathering activities of the federal government, along with the government's increasing use of new computer technologies to disseminate that information, pose a significant threat to the individual's right to privacy.[1]

In response to this threat, Congress has enacted several federal statutes that relate to the privacy of records containing information about individuals. These laws have significantly expanded and extended the right to privacy articulated by the Supreme Court. In fact, several of these new laws resulted from an adverse Congressional reaction to Supreme Court cases that had limited the right to privacy.

Many privacy laws also grew out of well-publicized instances of abuse of power by federal agencies and departments. However, the attempt to pass a national law to protect the privacy of library records failed, although it apparently had wide support in Congress.

PRIVACY STATUTES

Efforts by Congress to establish rules on the use and dissemination of government records began in the 1970s. While these laws cover a wide range of government activities, they still represent only a beginning.[2]

Fair Credit Reporting Act of 1970

The first privacy act passed by Congress concerned records compiled by credit and investigative reporting agencies. The Fair Credit Reporting Act:

- allows disclosure of credit records only to authorized customers;
- makes the records available to the person whose record it is;
- establishes procedures for correcting inaccurate information in the record.

Family Education Rights and Privacy Act of 1974

Four years later, Congress enacted the Buckley Amendment, which:

- required schools and colleges to allow students to have access to their own records;
- established procedures to challenge or correct those records; and
- limited the disclosure of student records to third parties.

Privacy Act of 1974

Later that year, Congress enacted the first comprehensive legislation to protect the confidentiality of personal information stored by federal agencies. The driving force behind this act was the growing computerization of government records about individuals. The act also was an outgrowth of a concrete incident.

During the Vietnam era, army agents were sent throughout the country to conduct surveillance on civilians who expressed their dissatisfaction with government policies. According to a Senate Judiciary Committee report, "In churches, on campuses, in public meetings, they took notes, tape recorded, and photographed people who dissented in thought, word or deed. This included clergymen, editors, public officials, and anyone who sympathized with the dissenters."[3] They monitored the membership and policies of peaceful organizations concerned with the war, the draft, and racial and labor problems. The Army created blacklists of organizations and personalities, which were circulated to many federal, state, and local agencies. The Senate's report states:

The Army did not just collect and share this information. Analysts were assigned the task of evaluating and labeling these people on the basis of reports on their attitudes,remarks and activities. They were then coded for entry into computers or microfilm data banks. . . . Despite First Amendment rights of Americans, and despite the constitutional division of power between the federal and state governments, despite laws and decisions defining the legal role and duties of the Army, the Army was given the power to create an information system of data banks and computer programs which threatened to erode these restrictions on governmental power.

The Privacy Act was enacted to prevent such abuse of government power. The act:

- requires each federal agency to publish a description of each system of records maintained by them that contains personal information;
- allows individuals to seek access to records about themselves and to challenge their accuracy;
- requires that information acquired for one purpose not be used for another purpose; and
- restricts disclosure of personally identifiable information by federal agencies.

The act attempts to prevent the secret gathering of information on individuals or the creation of secret information systems or databases on Americans.

The overall stated purpose of the Privacy Act is to promote respect for the privacy of citizens among all departments and agencies in the executive branch of government.[4] Its statement of purpose (see Appendix D) acknowledges that the right to privacy is a fundamental right protected by the Constitution. The act also requires federal agencies and departments to observe constitutional rules in the computerization, collection, management, use, and disclosure of personal information about individuals.[5] The act accomplishes these purposes in the following ways:

1. It requires agencies to give detailed notice of the nature and uses of their personal data banks.
2. It establishes minimum information-gathering standards for all agencies to protect the privacy of the individual.
3. It establishes minimum standards for handling and processing personal information in the data banks of the executive branch.
4. It provides for administrative and judicial oversight and civil remedies for violations.
5. It provides for a study of major data banks to recommend changes. The act also requires that agencies maintain no record describing how any

individual exercises rights guaranteed by the First Amendment unless expressly authorized by statute or by the individual about whom the record is maintained or unless pertinent to and within the scope of an authorized law-enforcement activity.

Tax Reform Act of 1976

Provisions of the act protect the confidentiality of individual tax returns and limit their disclosure primarily to federal and state tax authorities.

Right to Financial Privacy Act of 1978

As a response to a U.S. Supreme Court decision,[6] Congress enacted this legislation to establish an affirmative privacy interest in personal financial records. The act provides individuals with the right to be notified and to challenge a request for information before a bank or other financial institution may disclose records to government agencies.

Privacy Protection Act of 1980

This act prohibits law-enforcement agents from searching press offices if no one in the office is suspected of committing a crime. It also was enacted in reaction to a U.S. Supreme Court discussion.[7]

Electronic Funds Transfer Act of 1980

This act requires any institution providing electronic funds transfer or other bank services to notify its customers about third-party access to their accounts.

Fair Debt Collection Act of 1982

This act requires federal agencies to meet certain due process requirements before releasing debt information about an individual to a private credit bureau.

Cable Communications Policy Act of 1984

This act prohibits a cable service from disclosing information about a subscriber's cable viewing rights without the individual's consent. The act requires the cable service to inform the subscriber of:

- the nature and use of personally identifiable information collected;
- disclosures that will be made of such information;
- the period during which such information will be maintained; and
- access to the information maintained about them.

Electronic Communications Privacy Act

This act amended the federal wiretapping statute to prohibit the unauthorized interception and disclosure of electronic communications made possible by new technologies such as cellular phones, electronic mail and satellite television transmissions. The act:

- defines electronic communications;
- restricts disclosure of stored communications; and
- creates civil and criminal penalties for individuals who, without authorization, willfully intercept or disclose the contents of electronic communications or who access such communications while in electronic storage.

Computer Matching and Privacy Protection Act of 1988

This act extends the provisions of the 1974 Privacy Act to also cover computerized matching of personal information in federal agency databases.

LIBRARY RECORDS

On May 10, 1988, Senate Bill 2361 was introduced by its sponsors, Senators Patrick Leahy, Charles Grassley, Paul Simon, and Alan Simpson. The bill was entitled: "The Video and Library Privacy Protection Act of 1988" (see Appendix E). Senator Leahy stated that the purpose of the bill was to "ensure that the choice of books we read and the movies we view will be protected against unlawful disclosure."[8]

Background

The bill actually grew out of an incident that occurred during the nomination hearings of Judge Robert Bork for Justice of the Supreme Court. A reporter obtained a list of the video tapes Judge Bork and his family rented at a local video store and disclosed the list in a published newspaper article. In his introduction of the bill to the Senate, Senator Leahy prefaced his remarks by saying: "I joined with members of the Judiciary Committee and others in denouncing this unwarranted invasion of personal privacy. I said at the time this story broke and I repeat today that it is no one's business what video tapes Judge Bork or anyone else chooses to view."[9]

The Senator's introduction, in which he explains the purpose of the bill, echoes the language of the Supreme Court in recognizing the constitutional right to privacy(see chapter 3):

> Commentators and courts have struggled with the meaning of a "right to privacy." Some have said that it is the right of autonomy or personhood. Others have described it as the freedom from outside intrusion. Justice Brandeis said simply that it is the "right to be let alone."

> In practical terms our right to privacy protects the choice of movies we watch with our family in our own homes. And it protects the selection of books that we choose to read. These activities are at the core of any definition of personhood. They reveal our likes and dislikes, our interests and our whims. They say a great deal about our dreams and ambitions, our fears and our hopes. They reflect our individuality, and they describe us as people.

Senator Leahy then asks the questions: Who could have imagined that the video tapes one watches at home or the books that one reads in the evening might become matters of public record? He notes that even George Orwell would not have anticipated this.

The Senator points out that people have a reasonable expectation of privacy in the tapes they rent and the books they borrow from the library. While they might expect that video dealers exchange mailing lists, he says, "they do not expect, and what the law should not allow, is that a detailed list of their previous rentals—the titles of the films, the dates they were rented—will be disclosed to others, without their consent."[10]

Senator Leahy outlines the principal features of the bill as follows:

> [T]he principle behind this bill is a simple one: A person maintains a privacy interest in the transactional information about his or her personal activities. The disclosure of this information should only be permissible under well-defined circumstances."[11]

- Disclosure of video rental records and library borrower records is prohibited except to the borrower, to another with the borrower's consent, or under court order.
- Any borrower who is aggrieved by a violation may bring a civil action for damages.
- Video stores are permitted to sell customer lists, but cannot disclose the particular films their customers rented.

- Information about borrowers that is unlawfully obtained cannot be used in court proceedings.
- The bill requires the destruction of personal information one year from the date the information is no longer necessary for the purpose it was collected.

In his closing remarks, Senator Leahy said that he looked forward to working with video dealers and the library associations in strengthening privacy protection for their customers and patrons: "I applaud efforts that have already been taken by trade associations, professional groups, and others to establish information privacy protection with confidentiality provisions, record destruction policies, and enhanced security for automated systems containing personal information. All of these measures help safeguard the right of information privacy."[12] The Senator concluded his introduction by stating: "This bill is a significant step in extending the right of privacy, and, in so doing, makes each of us a little freer to read and watch what we choose without public scrutiny, and once again strengthens the rights of individual liberty that lie at the heart of our system of government."[13]

Effect on state statutes

Senator Grassley, in his introduction of the bill, stated that it is the function of the legislature to define, expand, and give meaning to the concept of privacy. Toward that end, "This bill will give specific meaning to the right of privacy, as it affects individuals in their daily lives."[14]

Senator Grassley discussed the relationship between this bill and state laws protecting the privacy of library records: "We do not want to preempt the States from acting in this area. In fact, the State legislators are particularly well suited to respond to technological changes and trends in society. Thus, under our bill, citizens in States with similar legislation will merely have an alternative in the Federal Remedy."[15]

Penalties

Senator Grassley also discussed the issue of penalties. Under this bill libraries that unlawfully disclose library records could have civil action brought against them in U.S. District Court. Libraries would be liable for actual and punitive damages, attorneys' fees, and equitable reliefs. Senator Grassley said that he shared a concern about imposing penalties on libraries, but "privacy, as defined in this bill, requires protection."[16] He also expected that library managers would educate their employees to minimize the possibility of unauthorized disclosure. The Senator concluded his introduction by stating: "Passage of this legislation will help define and as a result, enhance individual privacy."[17]

Exceptions

Senator Paul Simon spoke in his introduction of the bill, the exceptions to nondisclosure: "Since there are certain circumstances in which it may be necessary for this information to be divulged, the bill provides for some limited exceptions to the prohibition, including an exemption to cover legitimate law-enforcement activities."[18]

Under this bill, a library could reveal personally identifiable information concerning any patron:

- to the patron;
- to any person with the informed written consent of the patron given at the time of the disclosure;
- to a law-enforcement agency pursuant to a court order if the patron is given reasonable notice and opportunity to appear and contest the claim, and if the law-enforcement agency offers clear and convincing evidence that the patron is reasonably suspected of engaging in criminal activity and that the information sought is highly material to the case;
- to any person if the disclosure is only of the names and addresses of patrons and if the patron has been provided with a written statement that could prohibit the disclosure, and there is no disclosure of title, description, or subject matter of any library materials borrowed or used;
- to any authorized person if the disclosure is necessary for recovering the material or its value;
- pursuant to a court order in a civil action if the information cannot be obtained in any other way, and if the patron is given reasonable notice and opportunity to contest the claim.

Reaction to the bill

Library organizations generally supported the bill when it was introduced. Since 1970 the American Library Association (ALA) had a policy that library circulation records are confidential in nature and should not be revealed to any other party except in response to a valid court order.[19] ALA also felt that a court order obtained upon the showing of good cause before the appropriate judicial authority is the proper vehicle for obtaining library records.[20]

Amendments

ALA and other library organizations were, however, opposed to an amendment that surfaced after the bill was introduced. The amendment called for a creation of a "national security letter" disclosure process. The adoption of such a process would, in effect, authorize a part of the FBI Awareness Program or similar activities. Disputes over this amendment ultimately resulted in the deletion of the library record provisions from the bill which was then passed as the Video Privacy Protection Act of 1988 (see Appendix F).

We must now turn to state protection of library records.

Notes

1. Senator Sam Ervin in Senate Report (Government Operations Committee) No. 93-1183, September 26, 1974(to accompany S.3418), p.6.
2. Senate Report (Judiciary Committee) No. 100-599, October 5, 1988 [To accompany S. 2361], p.2.
3. Ibid. at p.17.
4. Ibid.
5. Senate Report(Government Operations Committee)No. 93-1183, September 26, 1974[To Accompany S.3418], p.1.
6. *U.S. v. Miller*, 425 U.S. 35(1976).
7. *Zurcher v. Stanford Daily*, 436 U.S. 547(1978).
8. *Congressional Record*, May 10, 1988, p.10259.
9. Ibid.
10. Ibid.
11. Ibid. at 10260.
12. Ibid.
13. Ibid.
14. Ibid. at 10261.
15. Ibid.
16. Ibid.
17. Ibid.
18. Ibid. at 10262.
19. Letter to Don Edwards from the American Library Association reprinted in *FBI Counterintelligence Visits to Libraries: Hearings before the Subcommittee on Civil Rights of the Committee on the Judiciary, House of Representatives, 100 Cong., 2d sess., June 20 and July 13, 1988* (Serial No. 123), p.399.
20. Ibid.

PART II

State Protection of the Privacy of Library Records

5

State Laws

The basis for the the confidentiality of library records is deeply rooted in the First Amendment and in the penumbral constitutional rights to seek information and ideas, to enjoy freedom of association, and privacy. The right of access to a library includes the right of freedom from government interference in the selection of library materials. These inferred constitutional rights, however, must be further defined and enacted by state statute.

STATE RECORDS

In this section, we examine the state laws that relate to the privacy of library records. To compare state library records confidentiality laws, it was necessary to establish an orderly arrangement of elements for comparison, identifying those items of most importance to our readers. Although the state laws vary, there are a number of states with similar laws. Therefore, the analyses that precede the text of each statute were developed to accommodate the greater number of states, as well as to summarize the information that is most pertinent to libraries. The subjects include:

- *the types of libraries covered by confidentiality laws,*
- *the types of records protected, and*
- *the instances in which the records may be released.*

(Tables 1 and 2 tabulate this information for easy reference.)

Anyone familiar with the making of laws recognizes it is not always easy to ascertain what the legislature intended when a law was written. The language of the law itself may leave a void in terms of how to interpret a word or phrase. A good example is the frequent use of such simple words as *library* or *libraries* without defining

Library Records Confidentiality--What Records are Protected?

State	Law	Registration	Circulation	Materials used in Library	Personally identifiable info	Info Requests	Service Request
AL	Yes	Yes	Yes	Yes	Yes		
AS	Yes		Yes	Yes	Yes		Yes
AZ	Yes	Yes	Yes	Yes	Yes		Yes
AK	Yes	Yes	Yes	Yes	Yes	Yes	
CA	Yes	Yes	Yes		Yes		
CO	Yes	Yes	Yes	Yes	Yes	Yes	Yes
CT	Yes	Yes	Yes		Yes		
DE	Yes	Yes	Yes	Yes	Yes		
DC	Yes		Yes	Yes	Yes		Yes
FL	Yes	Yes	Yes	Yes	Yes		
GA	Yes	Yes	Yes	Yes	Yes		
HA	No	Yes		Yes	Yes	Yes	Yes
ID	Yes	Yes	Yes	Yes	Yes		
IL	Yes	Yes	Yes		Yes		
IN	Yes	Yes	Yes	Yes	Yes	Yes	Yes
IO	Yes	Yes	Yes	Yes	Yes	Yes	
KA	Yes	Yes	Yes	Yes			
KY	No						
LA	Yes	Yes	Yes	Yes	Yes		
ME	Yes	Yes	Yes	Yes	Yes		
MD	Yes	Yes	Yes	Yes	Yes	Yes	Yes
MA	Yes	Yes	Yes	Yes	Yes	Yes	Yes
MI	Yes	Yes	Yes	Yes	Yes		
MN	Yes	Yes	Yes	Yes	Yes	Yes	Yes

State	1	2	3	4	5	6	7
MS			Yes	Yes	Yes	Yes	Yes
MO	Yes	Yes	Yes	Yes	Yes	Yes	Yes
MT		Yes	Yes	Yes	Yes	Yes	Yes
NE	Yes	Yes	Yes	Yes	Yes	Yes	Yes
NV			Yes	Yes	Yes	Yes	Yes
NH		Yes	Yes	Yes	Yes	Yes	Yes
NJ			Yes	Yes	Yes	Yes	Yes
NM			Yes	Yes	Yes	Yes	Yes
NY			Yes	Yes	Yes	Yes	Yes
NC		Yes	Yes	Yes	Yes	Yes	Yes
ND		Yes	Yes	Yes	Yes	Yes	Yes
OH			Yes				No
OK			Yes				Yes
OR			Yes				Yes
PA			Yes	Yes	Yes	Yes	Yes
RI	Yes	Yes	Yes	Yes	Yes	Yes	Yes
SC		Yes	Yes	Yes	Yes	Yes	Yes
SD	Yes		Yes	Yes	Yes	Yes	Yes
TN			Yes	Yes	Yes	Yes	Yes
TX			Yes				No
VT			Yes	Yes	Yes	Yes	Yes
UT			Yes	Yes	Yes	Yes	Yes
VA			Yes	Yes	Yes	Yes	Yes
WA			Yes	Yes	Yes	Yes	Yes
WV			Yes	Yes	Yes	Yes	Yes
WI			Yes	Yes	Yes	Yes	Yes
WY			Yes	Yes	Yes	Yes	Yes

Library Records Confidentiality--Which Libraries and What are the Exceptions?

State	Public Lib.	Public Acad. Lib.	Public School Lib.	Priv. Lib. Open to the Public	Any Lib. Using Public Funds	User Consent	Parent or guardian	Court Order or Subpoena
AL	Yes	Yes	Yes				Yes	
AS	Yes	Yes	Yes			Yes	Yes	Yes
AZ					Yes	Yes		Yes
AK					Yes	Yes		Yes
CA					Yes	Yes		Yes
CO					Yes	Yes		Yes
CT	Yes							
DE	Yes							
DC	Yes					Yes		Yes
FL	Yes							Yes
GA	Yes					Yes	Yes	Yes
HA								
ID	Yes							
IL	Yes	Yes	Yes					Yes
IN	Yes	Yes	Yes					Yes
IO	Yes							Yes
KA	Yes							
KY								
LA	Yes				Yes	Yes	Yes	
ME	Yes					Yes		Yes
MD	Yes	Yes						Yes
MA	Yes		Yes					
MI	Yes	Yes	Yes	Yes	Yes	Yes		Yes
MN	Yes	Yes	Yes					Yes

State	Col 1	Col 2	Col 3	Col 4	Col 5	Col 6	Col 7
MS	Yes	Yes	Yes	Yes	Yes		Yes
MO	Yes	Yes	Yes		Yes		Yes
MT					Yes		Yes
NE	Yes			Yes			
NV	Yes	Yes	Yes	Yes	Yes		Yes
NH	Yes	Yes	Yes	Yes	Yes		Yes
NJ	Yes	Yes		Yes	Yes		Yes
NM	Yes	Yes	Yes	Yes	Yes	Yes	Yes
NY	Yes	Yes	Yes	Yes	Yes		Yes
NC	Yes		Yes	Yes			Yes
ND							Yes
OH¹				Yes			
OK					Yes		Yes
OR							
PA	Yes	Yes			Yes		
RI	Yes				Yes		
SC	Yes	Yes		Yes	Yes		Yes
SD	Yes			Yes	Yes	Yes	Yes
TN	Yes	Yes	Yes	Yes			Yes
TX²							
VT	Yes						
UT	Yes						
VA				Yes			
WA							
WV	Yes			Yes	Yes		Yes
WI	Yes				Yes	Yes	Yes
WY	Yes						

1. Protected only through limited confidentiality and administrative policy.
2. Library records exempt because privacy is Constitionality protected.

which libraries they are meant to describe. If a law using this term is part of a state's public records law (the law allowing access to public records in that state, sometimes called *Sunshine Laws* or *Freedom of Information Laws*), then one can infer that the words *library* or *libraries* are meant to describe *publicly funded* libraries that would be considered public agencies whose records are public records. However, that is an inference and it may prove to be too all-encompassing, or sometimes, not encompassing enough. If the law in question is part of the state's library laws, then *public libraries* that serve individual municipalities may be the only intended institutions. Sometimes it is difficult to tell. Consequently, the analyses made here have stayed, for the most part, strictly with the words as stated in the laws. This means that the law's coverage may be broader than stated here, but it is not likely to be narrower.

Occasionally, it is simply not possible to ascertain what the law intends to do in a given area. This is particularly true with regard to what records are covered. As an example, in every case where a law exists, the patron registration and circulation files seem to be protected. However, it is generally not clear whether or not the use of materials by a patron within the library is a protected activity. This situation probably comes about because legislators are not familiar with the fact that patrons often must ask for help in finding material that they need to refer to in-house and that the librarian helping them may either know already or inquire as to the patron's name.

To ensure the confidentiality of library-records, most states passed either an amendment to the state freedom of information law or they created a section within the state's library laws.

STATE LAWS

Alabama   **Year of Passage: 1983**

Type of Law:

      __Part of state records-access law
      x Separate law specific to libraries
      __No law on confidentiality of library records

Types of Libraries covered:

> <u>x</u> **Public Libraries**
> <u>x</u> **Public Academic**
> <u>x</u> **Public Schools**
> __Library Systems
> __Private Libraries open to the public
> __Any library using public funds

Covered Records:

> <u>x</u> **Patron Registration**
> <u>x</u> **Circulation Records**
> <u>x</u> **Use of Materials in Library**
> __Information Queries
> __Requests for Materials
> __Requests for Services

Law Defines Terms? **Yes** No

When information contained in library records may be released:

> __With user consent
> [Consent must be in writing __Yes __No __Unclear]
> <u>x</u> **Parent or guardian of minor seeks records of that minor**
> <u>x</u> **For library operation**
> __Pursuant to a court order or subpoena
> <u>x</u> **State Library request**
> <u>x</u> **Education Department Request**

Remarks: The State Library and the Education Department may only have access to the records for a library under their jurisdiction when it is necessary to assure the proper operation of such library.

There is no reference in this part of the law to user consent or court orders or subpoenas as a way to gain access.

Text of Law:

Act No. 83-565   S.322 — Senators Little and Mitchem

AN ACT

To provide for the confidentiality of circulation and registration records maintained by public school libraries, public

libraries and college and university libraries; and to amend Section 36-12-40, Code of Alabama 1975, so as to provide for said exemption and to provide certain exceptions.

Be It Enacted by the Legislature of Alabama:

Section 1. As used in the following section, the term "registration records" includes any information which a library requires a patron to provide in order to become eligible to borrow books and other materials, and the term "circulation records" includes all information which identifies the patrons utilizing particular books and any other library materials in any medium or format.

Section 2. It is recognized that public library use by an individual should be of confidential nature. Any other provision of general, special or local law, rule or regulation to the contrary notwithstanding, the registration and circulation records and information concerning the use of the public, public school, college and university libraries of this state shall be confidential. Registration and circulation records shall not be open for inspection by, or otherwise available to, any agency or individual except for the following entities: (a) the library which manages the records; (b) the state education department for a library under its jurisdiction when it is necessary to assure the proper operation of such library; or (c) the state public library service for a library under its jurisdiction when it is necessary to assure the proper operation of such library. Aggregate statistics shown from registration and circulation records, with all personal identification removed, may be released or used by a library for research and planning purposes. Provided however, any parent of a minor child shall have the right to inspect the registration and circulation records of any school or public library that pertains to his or her child.

Section 3. Section 36-12-40, Code of Alabama 1975, is hereby amended to read as follows:

"Section 36-12-40. Every citizen has a right to inspect and take a copy of any public writing of this state, except as otherwise expressly provided by statute. Provided however, registration and circulation records and information concerning the use of the public, public school or college and university libraries of this state shall be exempt from this section." Provided further, any parent of a minor child shall have the right to inspect the registration and circulation records of any school or public library that pertain to his or her child.

Section 4. All laws or parts of law which conflict with this act are hereby repealed.

Section 5. This act shall become effective immediately upon its passage and approval by the Governor, or upon its otherwise becoming a law.

Approved July 18, 1983

Time: 2:15 P.M.

Alaska   **Year of Passage: 1985**

Type of Law:

    _Part of state records access law
    x Separate law specific to libraries
    _No law on confidentiality of library records

Types of Libraries covered:

    x Public Libraries
    x Public Academic
    x Public Schools
    _Library Systems
    _Private Libraries open to the public
    _Any library using public funds

Covered Records:

    x Patron Registration
    x Circulation Records
    _Use of Materials in Library
    _Information Queries
    _Requests for Materials
    _Requests for Services

Law Defines Terms? Yes **No**

When information contained in library records may be released:

    _With user consent
    [Consent must be in writing _Yes _No _Unclear]
    x Parent or guardian of minor seeks records of that minor
    _For library operation
    x Pursuant to a court order or subpoena
    _State Library request
    _Education Department Request

Remarks: The records covered are those which contain the names, addresses or other personal identifying information of people who have used materials made available to the public by a library. The libraries covered are those operated by the state, a municipality or public school, including the University of Alaska.

Text of Law:

Chapter 35

AN ACT

Relating to the confidentiality of certain library records.

Section 1. AS 09.25 is amended by adding a new section to read:

Section 09.25.140. CONFIDENTIALITY OF LIBRARY RECORDS. (a)Except as provided in (b) of this section, the names, addresses, or other personal identifying information of people who have used materials made available to the public by a library shall be kept confidential, except upon court order, and not subject to inspection under AS 09.25.110 or 09.25.120. This section applies to libraries operated by the state, a municipality, or a public school, including the University of Alaska.

(b)Records of a public elementary or secondary school library identifying a minor child shall be made available on request to a parent or guardian of that child.

Arizona   **Year of Passage: 1985**

Type of Law:

      _Part of state records access law
      x Separate law specific to libraries
      _No law on confidentiality of library records

Types of Libraries covered:

      _Public Libraries
      _Public Academic
      _Public Schools
      _Library Systems
      _Private Libraries open to the public

x Any library using public funds

Covered Records:

x Patron Registration
x Circulation Records
x Use of Materials in Library
x Information Queries
x Requests for Materials
x Requests for Services

Law Defines Terms? **x Yes** __No

When information contained in library records may be released:

x With user consent
  [Consent must be in writing **x Yes** __No __Unclear]
  __Parent or guardian of minor seeks records of that minor
x For library operation
x Pursuant to a court order or subpoena
  __State Library request
  __Education Department Request

Remarks: In addition to allowing access on receipt of a court order, the law speaks of access being available "if required by law."

Text of Law:

PUBLIC LIBRARIES—PRIVACY OF USER RECORDS

CHAPTER 69

HOUSE BILL 2317

AN ACT

RELATING TO STATE GOVERNMENT; PROVIDING FOR PRIVACY OF RECORDS FOR USERS OF PUBLIC LIBRARIES OR LIBRARY SYSTEM; PRESCRIBING EXCEPTIONS TO PRIVACY; PRESCRIBING DEFINITION AND CLASSIFICATION OF CERTAIN CRIMINAL OFFENSE, AND AMENDING TITLE 41, CHAPTER 8, ARTICLE 3, ARIZONA REVISED STATUTES, BY ADDING SECTION 41-1354.

Be it enacted by the Legislature of the State of Arizona:

Section 1. Title 41, chapter 8, article 3, Arizona Revised Statutes, is amended by adding section 41-1354, to read:

41-1354. *Privacy of user records; exceptions; violation; classification*

A. EXCEPT AS PROVIDED IN SUBSECTION B, A LIBRARY OR LIBRARY SYSTEM SUPPORTED BY PUBLIC MONIES SHALL NOT ALLOW DISCLOSURE OF ANY RECORD OR OTHER INFORMATION WHICH IDENTIFIES A USER OF LIBRARY SERVICES AS REQUESTING OR OBTAINING SPECIFIC MATERIALS OR SERVICES OR AS OTHERWISE USING THE LIBRARY.

B. RECORDS MAY BE DISCLOSED:

1. IF NECESSARY FOR THE REASONABLE OPERATION OF THE LIBRARY.

2. ON WRITTEN CONSENT OF THE USER.

3. ON RECEIPT OF A COURT ORDER.

4. IF REQUIRED BY LAW.

C. ANY PERSON WHO KNOWINGLY DISCLOSES ANY RECORD OR OTHER INFORMATION IN VIOLATION OF THIS SECTION IS GUILTY OF A CLASS 3 MISDEMEANOR.

Approved by the Governor, April 9, 1985.

Filed in the Office of the Secretary of State, April 9, 1985.

Arkansas   **Year of Passage: 1989**

Type of Law:

  __Part of state records access law
  x Separate law specific to libraries
  __No law on confidentiality of library records

Types of Libraries covered:

  __Public Libraries
  __Public Academic
  __Public Schools
  __Library Systems
  __Private Libraries open to the public
  x Any library using public funds

Covered Records:

     x Patron Registration
     x Circulation Records
     x Use of Materials in Library
     x Information Queries
     x Requests for Materials
     x Requests for Services

Law Defines Terms? **x Yes** __No

When information contained in library records may be released:

     x With user consent
     [Consent must be in writing **x Yes** __No __Unclear]
     __Parent or guardian of minor seeks records of that minor
     x For library operation
     x Pursuant to a court order or subpoena
     __State Library request
     __Education Department Request

Remarks: The Arkansas law prohibits personally identifiable library record information obtained in any other manner than as provided therein from being received in evidence in either a court trial or an administrative proceeding. It states that the patron has access to his or her own records.

Text of Law:

ACT 903

AN ACT to Provide that Library Records Containing Names or Other

Personally Identifying Details Regarding the Patrons of the Library Shall be Confidential; and for Other Purposes.

Be It Enacted by the General Assembly of the State of Arkansas:

SECTION 1.(a) "patron" means any individual who requests, uses, or receives services, books or other materials from a library.

(b) "Confidential library records" means documents or information in any format retained in a library that identify a patron as having requested, used, or obtained specific materials including, but not limited to, circulation of library books, materials, computer data base searches, interlibrary loan transactions, reference queries, patent searches, requests for photocopies of library materials, title reserve requests, or the use of audiovisual materials, films or records.

SECTION 2.(a) Library records which contain names or other personally identifying details regarding the patrons of public, school, academic, and special libraries and library systems supported in whole or in part by public funds shall be confidential and shall not be disclosed except as permitted by this act.

(b) A library may disclose personally identifiable information concerning any patron:

(1) To the patron;

(2) To any person with the informed, written consent of the patron given at the time the disclosure is sought; or

(3) To a law enforcement agency or civil court, pursuant to a search warrant.

(c) Personally identifiable information obtained in any manner other than as provided in this subchapter shall not be received in evidence in any trial, hearing, arbitration, or other proceeding before any court, grand jury, department, officer, agency, regulatory body, legislative committee, or other authority of the state or political subdivision of the state.

(d) No provision of this subchapter shall be construed to prohibit any library or any business operating jointly with a library from disclosing information for the purpose of collecting overdue books, documents, films, or other items or materials owned or otherwise belonging to such library. Nor shall any provision of this subchapter be construed as to prohibit or hinder any such library or business office from collecting fines on such overdue books, documents, films, or other items or materials.

(e) Aggregate statistics shown from registration and circulation records with all personal identification removed may be released or used by a library or library system for research or planning purposes.

(f) Any person who knowingly violates any of the provisions of this subchapter shall be guilty of a misdemeanor and shall be punished by a fine of no more than two hundred dollars($200) or thirty(30) days in jail, or both, or a sentence of appropriate public service or education, or both.

(g) No liability shall result from any lawful disclosure permitted by this subchapter.

(h) No action may be brought under this subchapter unless such action is begun within two(2) years from the date of the act complained of or the date of discovery.

(i) Public libraries shall use an automated or Gaylord-type circulation system that does not identify a patron with circulated materials after materials are returned.

SECTION 3. All provisions of this act of a general and permanent nature are amendatory to the Arkansas Code of 1987 Annotated and the Arkansas Code Revision Commission shall incorporate the same in the Code.

SECTION 4. All laws and parts of laws in conflict with this act are hereby repealed.

APPROVED: March 23, 1989.

California   **Year of Passage: 1986**

Type of Law:

       _Part of state records access law
       x Separate law specific to libraries
       _No law on confidentiality of library records

Types of Libraries covered:

       _Public Libraries
       _Public Academic
       _Public Schools
       _Library Systems
       _Private Libraries open to the public
       x Any library using public funds

Covered Records:

       x Patron Registration
       x Circulation Records
       _Use of Materials in Library

_Information Queries
_Requests for Materials
_Requests for Services

Law Defines Terms? _Yes x No

When information contained in library records may be released:

x With user consent
   [Consent must be in writing **x Yes** _No _Unclear]
   _Parent or guardian of minor seeks records of that minor
x For library operation
x Pursuant to a court order or subpoena
   _State Library request
   _Education Department Request

Text of Law:

An act to add Section 6267 to the Government Code, relating to library records.

[Approved by Governor June 17, 1986. Filed with Secretary of State June 18, 1986]

The people of the State of California do enact as follows:

SECTION 1. Section 6267 is added to the Government Code, to read:

6267. All registration and circulation records of any library which is in whole or in part supported by public funds shall remain confidential and shall not be disclosed to any person, local agency, or state agency except as follows:

(a) By a person acting within the scope of his or her duties within the administration of the library.

(b) By a person authorized, in writing, by the individual to whom the records pertain, to inspect the records.

(c) By order of the appropriate superior court.

As used in this section, the term "registration records" includes any information which a library requires a patron to provide in order to become eligible to borrow books and other materials, and the term "circulation records" includes any information which identifies the patrons borrowing particular books and other material.

This section shall not apply to statistical reports of registration and circulation nor to records of fines collected by the library.

Colorado   **Year of Passage: 1983**

Type of Law:

     __Part of state records access law
     x Separate law specific to libraries
     __No law on confidentiality of library records

Types of Libraries covered:

     __Public Libraries
     __Public Academic
     __Public Schools
     __Library Systems
     __Private Libraries open to the public
     x Any library using public funds

Covered Records:

     x Patron Registration
     x Circulation Records
     x Use of Materials in Library
     x Information Queries
     x Requests for Materials
     x Requests for Services

Law Defines Terms? __Yes **x No**

When information contained in library records may be released:

     x With user consent
       [Consent must be in writing **x Yes** __No __Unclear]
     __Parent or guardian of minor seeks records of that minor
     x For library operation
     x Pursuant to a court order or subpoena
     __State Library request
     __Education Department Request

Text of Law:

Chapter 297

———

GOVERNMENT—STATE

LIBRARIES—LIBRARY LAW

———

HOUSE BILL NO. 1114. BY REPRESENTATIVES Paulson, Armstrong, Bath, Campbell, Castro, Davoren, DeFilippo, Fine, Groff, Herzog, Hover, Hume, Knox, Lee, Lucero, Martinez, Moore, Neale, Robb, Strahle, Taylor, Tebedo, Truijillo and Webb; also SENATORS Traylor, Baca Brandon, Gallagher, and Stewart.

AN ACT

CONCERNING PRIVACY OF LIBRARY USER RECORDS.

Be it enacted by the General Assembly of the State of Colorado:

Section 1. Part 1 of article 90 of title 24, Colorado Revised Statutes 1973, 1982 Repl. Vol., is amended BY THE ADDITION OF A NEW SECTION to read:

24-90-119. Privacy of user records. (1) Except as set forth in subsection (2) of this section, a publicly-supported library or library system shall not disclose any record or other information which identifies a person as having requested or obtained specific materials or service or as otherwise having used the library.

(2) Records may be disclosed in the following instances:

(a) When necessary for the reasonable operation of the library;

(b) Upon written consent of the user;

(c) Pursuant to subpoena, upon court order, or where otherwise required by law.

(3) Any library or library system official, employee, or volunteer who discloses information in violation of this section commits a class 2 petty offense and, upon conviction thereof, shall be punished by a fine of not more than three hundred dollars.

Section 2 24-72-204(3)(a)(V) and (3)(a)(VI), Colorado Revised Statutes 1973, 1982 Repl. Vol., are amended and the said 24-72-204(3)(a) is further amended BY THE ADDITION OF A NEW SUBPARAGRAPH, to read:

24-72-204. Allowance or denial of inspection - grounds -

procedures - appeal. (3)(a)(V) Library and museum material contributed by private persons, to the extent of any limitations placed thereon as conditions of such contributions; and

(VI) Addresses and telephone numbers of students in any public elementary or secondary school; AND

(VII) Library records disclosing the identity of a user as prohibited by section 24-90-119.

Section 3. Safety clause. The general assembly hereby finds, determines, and declares that this act is necessary for the immediate preservation of the public peace, health, and safety.

Approved: March 22, 1983

Connecticut   **Year of Passage: 1981**

Type of Law:

       __Part of state records access law
       x Separate law specific to libraries
       __No law on confidentiality of library records

Types of Libraries covered:

       x Public Libraries
       __Public Academic
       __Public Schools
       __Library Systems
       __Private Libraries open to the public
       __Any library using public funds

Covered Records:

       __Patron Registration
       x Circulation Records
       __Use of Materials in Library
       __Information Queries
       __Requests for Materials
       __Requests for Services

Law Defines Terms? __Yes **x No**

When information contained in library records may be released:

__With user consent
   [Consent must be in writing __Yes __No __Unclear]
__Parent or guardian of minor seeks records of that minor
__For library operation
x **Pursuant to a court order or subpoena**
__State Library request
__Education Department Request

Remarks: The Connecticut law is the briefest of those passed as a library law. It was interpreted in an opinion letter of an assistant attorney general, who stressed that it represented only his own opinion. According to this letter, only library circulation records are covered, and disclosure to parents or guardians of their minor children is not prohibited since they are not the *public*.

Text of Law:

[P.A. 81-431, sec. 16]

(a) The libraries established under the provisions of this chapter, and any free public library receiving a state appropriation, shall annually make a report to the state library board.

(b) Notwithstanding the provisions of section 1-19, personally identifiable information contained in the circulation records of all public libraries shall be confidential.

Delaware   **Year of Passage: 1981**

Type of Law:

   x **Part of state records access law**
   __Separate law specific to libraries
   __No law on confidentiality of library records

Types of Libraries covered:

   x **Public Libraries**

__Public Academic
__Public Schools
__Library Systems
__Private Libraries open to the public
__Any library using public funds

Covered Records:

x Patron Registration
x Circulation Records
x Use of Materials in Library
__Information Queries
x Requests for Materials
__Requests for Services

Law Defines Terms? **x Yes** __No

When information contained in library records may be released:

__With user consent
  [Consent must be in writing __Yes __No __Unclear]
__Parent or guardian of minor seeks records of that minor
__For library operation
__Pursuant to a court order or subpoena
__State Library request
__Education Department Request

Text of Law:

Chapter 100. Freedom Of Information Act

§10002. Definitions.

*. . .

(d)"Public record" is information of any kind, owned, made, used, retained, received, produced, composed, drafted or otherwise compiled or collected, by any public body, relating in any way to public business, or in any way of public interest, or in any way related to public purposes, regardless of the physical form or characteristic by which such information is stored, recorded or reproduced. For the purposes of this chapter, the following records shall not be deemed public:

(12)Any records of a public library which contain the identity of a user and the books, documents, films, recordings or other property of the library which a patron has used.

District of Columbia   **Year of Passage: 1985**

Type of Law:

    _Part of state records access law
    x Separate law specific to libraries
    _No law on confidentiality of library records

Types of Libraries covered:

    x Public Library
    _Public Academic
    _Public Schools
    _Library Systems
    _Private Libraries open to the public
    _Any library using public funds

Covered Records:

    x Patron Registration
    x Circulation Records
    x Use of Materials in Library
    _Information Queries
    x Requests for Materials
    _Requests for Services

Law Defines Terms? _Yes **x No**

When information contained in library records may be released:

    x With user consent
    [Consent must be in writing **x Yes** _No _Unclear]
    _Parent or guardian of minor seeks records of that minor
    x For library operation
    x Pursuant to a court order or subpoena
    _State Library request
    _Education Department Request

Remarks: The D.C. law requires that patrons whose records are subpoenaed be notified so that they may file, if they wish, a motion with the court requesting that the records not be released. However, there are circumstances under which this requirement if waived. Therefore, it is important for residents of the District of Columbia to be familiar with the library confidentiality law.

Text of Law:

D.C. LAW 5-128

DISTRICT OF COLUMBIA CONFIDENTIALITY OF LIBRARY RECORDS ACT OF

1984

IN THE COUNCIL OF THE DISTRICT OF COLUMBIA

March 13, 1985

To protect the confidentiality of District of Columbia public library records and to prohibit the officers, employees, and agents of the public library from disclosing circulation records of library patrons.

BE IT ENACTED BY THE COUNCIL OF THE DISTRICT OF COLUMBIA, That this act may be cited as the "District of Columbia Confidentiality of Library Records Act of 1984."

Section 2. An Act To establish and provide for the maintenance of a free public library and reading room in the District of Columbia, approved June 3, 1896 (29 Stat. 244; D.C. Code, sec. 37-101 et seq.), is amending by adding a new section 8 to read as follows:

Sec. 8.(a) Circulation records maintained by the public library in the District of Columbia which can be used to identify a library patron who has requested, used, or borrowed identified library materials from the public library and the specific material that patron has requested, used, or borrowed from the public library, shall be kept confidential, except that the records may be disclosed to officers, employees, and agents of the public library to the extent necessary for the proper operation of the public library.

"(b)(1) Circulation records shall not be disclosed by any officer, employee, or agent of the public library to a third party or parties, except with the written permission of the affected library patron or as the result of a court order.

　"(2) A person whose records are requested pursuant to paragraph (1) of this subsection may file a motion in the Superior Court of the District of Columbia requesting that the records be kept confidential. The motion shall be accompanied by their reasons for the request.

"(3) Paragraph (1) of this subsection shall not operate to prohibit the officers of the public library from disclosing relevant information on a library patron to the Corporate Counsel of the District of Columbia or legal counsel retained to represent the public library in a civil action.

"(4) Within 2 working days after receiving a subpoena issued by the court for public library records, the public library shall send a cop of the subpoena and the following notice, by certified mail, to all affected library patrons:

"Records or information concerning your borrowing records in the public library in the District of Columbia are being sought pursuant to the enclosed subpoena.

"In accordance with the District of Columbia Confidentiality of Library Records Act of 1984, these records will not be released until 10 days from the date this notice was mailed.

"If you desire that these records or information not be released, you must file a motion in the Superior Court of the District of Columbia requesting that the records be kept confidential, and state your reasons for the request. A sample motion is enclosed.

"You may wish to contact a lawyer. If you do not have a lawyer, you may call the District of Columbia Bar Lawyer Referral Service."

"(5) The public library shall not make available any subpoenaed materials until 10 days after the above notice has been mailed.

"(6) Upon application of a government authority, the notice required by paragraph (4) of this subsection may be waived by order of an appropriate court if the presiding judge finds that:

"(A) The investigation being conducted is within the lawful jurisdiction of the government authority seeking the records.

"(B) There is reason to believe that the records being sought are relevant to a legitimate law enforcement inquiry.

"(C) There is reason to believe that the notice will result in:

"(i) Endangering the life or physical safety of any person;

"(ii) Flight from prosecution;

"(iii) Destruction of or tampering with evidence;

"(iv) Intimidation of potential witnesses; or

"(v) Otherwise seriously jeopardizing an investigation or official proceeding.

"(7) The term "government authority", as used in paragraph (6) of this subsection, means any federal, state, or local government agency or department.

"(c) The Board of Library Trustees may issue rules necessary to implement this section.

"(d) Unless otherwise authorized or required by law, any officer, employee, or agent of the public library who shall violate any provision of this section or any rules issued pursuant to it commits a misdemeanor, and upon conviction shall be punished by a fine of not more than $300. The aggrieved public library patron may also bring a civil action against the individual violator for actual damages or $250, whichever is greater, reasonable attorneys' fees, and court costs.

Sec. 3. This act shall take effect after a 30-day period of Congressional review following approval by the Mayor (or in the event of veto by the Mayor, action by the Council of the District of Columbia to override the veto) as provided in section 602(c)(1) of the District of Columbia Self-Government and Governmental Reorganization Act, approved December 24, 1973 (87 Stat. 813; D.C. Code, sec. 1-233(c)(1)).

Source

Pursuant to Section 412 of the District of Columbia Self-Government and Government Reorganization Act, P.L. 93-198, "the Act", the Council of the District of Columbia adopted Bill No. 5-401 on first and second readings, July 10, 1984, and September 12, 1984, respectively. Following the signature of the Mayor on October 1, 1984, this legislation was assigned Act No. 5-181, published in the October 19, 1984 edition of the *D.C. Register*, (Vol. 31 page 5187) and transmitted to Congress January 7, 1985 for a 30-day review, in accordance with Section 602(c)(1) of the Act.

The Council of the District of Columbia hereby gives notice that the 30-day Congressional Review Period has expired, and therefore, cites this enactment as D.C. Law 5-128, effective March 13, 1985.

Florida   **Year of Passage: 1989**

Type of Law:

<u>x</u> **Part of state records access law**

_Separate law specific to libraries
_No law on confidentiality of library records

Types of Libraries covered:

x Public Libraries
_Public Academic
_Public Schools
_Library Systems
_Private Libraries open to the public
_Any library using public funds

Covered Records:

x Patron Registration
x Circulation Records
_Use of Materials in Library
_Information Queries
_Requests for Materials
_Requests for Services

Law Defines Terms? **x** _No

When information contained in library records may be released:

_With user consent
[Consent must be in writing _Yes _No _Unclear]
_Parent or guardian of minor seeks records of that minor
_For library operation
x Pursuant to a court order or subpoena
_State Library request
_Education Department Request

Text of Law:

CHAPTER 89-18

House Bill No. 1531

An act relating to library registration and circulation records; amending s. 257.261, F.S., which provides an exemption from public records requirements for library registration and circulation records; saving such exemption from repeal; providing for future review and repeal; providing an effective date.

Be It Enacted by the Legislature of the State of Florida:

Section 1. Notwithstanding the October 1, 1989 repeal in section 119.14(3)(a), Florida Statutes, section 257.261, Florida Statutes, is reenacted and amended to read:

257.261 Library registration and circulation records.—All registration and circulation records of every public library, except statistical reports of registration and circulation, shall be confidential *and exempt from the provision of s. 119.07(1)* information. Except in accordance with proper judicial order, no person shall make known in any manner any information contained in such records. As used in this section, the term "registration records" includes any information which a library requires a patron to provide in order to become eligible to borrow books and other materials, and the term "circulation records" includes all information which identifies the patrons borrowing particular books and other materials. Any person violating the provisions of this section is guilty of a misdemeanor of the second degree, punishable as provided in s. 775.082 *or*; s.775.03, or s. 775.084. *This exemption is subject to the Open Government Sunset Review Act in accordance with s. 119.14.*

Section 2. This act shall take effect October 1, 1989.

Approved by the Governor May 22, 1989.

Filed in Office Secretary of State May 22, 1989.

Georgia   **Year of Passage: 1987**

Type of Law:

> **x Part of state records access law**
> __Separate law specific to libraries
> __No law on confidentiality of library records

Types of Libraries covered:

> **x Public Libraries**
> __Public Academic
> __Public Schools

_Library Systems
_Private Libraries open to the public
_Any library using public funds

Covered Records:

x Patron Registration
x Circulation Records
_Use of Materials in Library
_Information Queries
_Requests for Materials
_Requests for Services

Law Defines Terms? _Yes **x No**

When information contained in library records may be released:

x With user consent
   [Consent must be in writing **x Yes** _No _Unclear]
**x Parent or guardian of minor seeks records of that
   minor**
x For library operation
x Pursuant to a court order or subpoena
_State Library request
_Education Department Request

Remarks: The language of the law itself is not specific in regard to what types of libraries are covered. It states that "circulation and similar records of a library which identify the user of library materials shall not be public records." One can presume that public libraries are covered. However, other types of libraries may also be covered by this law, depending on the legislature's intent.

Text of Law:

EVIDENCE—LIBRARY RECORDS; CONFIDENTIAL NATURE; DISCLOSURE; IMMUNITY.

Code Section 24-9-46 Enacted

AN ACT

To amend Article 2 of Chapter 9 of Title 24 of the Official Code of

Georgia Annotated, relating to privilege, so as to provide for the confidential nature of certain library records; to provide for disclosure of such records and for immunity from liability thereof; to repeal conflicting laws; and for other purposes.

BE IT ENACTED BY THE GENERAL ASSEMBLY OF GEORGIA:

Section 1. Article 2 of Chapter 9 of Title 24 of the Official Code of Georgia Annotated, relating to privilege, is amended by adding at the end thereof a new Code section to read as follows:

24-9-4. (a) Circulation and similar records of a library which identify the user of library materials shall not be public records but shall be confidential and may not be disclosed except:

> (1) To members of the library staff in the ordinary course of business;
> (2) Upon written consent of the user of the library materials or the user's parents or guardian if the user is a minor or ward; or
> (3) Upon appropriate court order or subpoena.

(b) Any disclosure authorized by subsection (a) of this Code section or any unauthorized disclosure of materials made confidential by that subsection (a) shall not in any way destroy the confidential nature of that material, except for the purpose for which an authorized disclosure is made. A person disclosing material as authorized by subsection (a) of this Code section shall not be liable therefor.

Section 2. All laws and parts of laws in conflict with this Act are repealed.

Approved April 2, 1987.

Hawaii

Hawaii does not have a specific statute that prohibits public access to public library records. However, in an October 23, 1990, advisory opinion addressed to the State Librarian, the Office of Information Practices stated that in their opinion "individuals have a significant privacy interest in information that reveals the materials that they have requested, used, or obtained from a public library" and that disclosure of such information would result in a clearly unwarranted invasion of personal privacy. An exception was noted for fines owed by individual for overdue books.

Idaho   Year of Passage: 1990

Type of Law:

> **x Part of state records access law**
> _Separate law specific to libraries
> _No law on confidentiality of library records

Types of Libraries covered:

> **x Public Libraries**
> _Public Academic
> _Public Schools
> _Library Systems
> _Private Libraries open to the public
> _Any library using public funds

Covered Records:

> **x Patron Registration**
> **x Circulation Records**
> **x Use of Materials in Library**
> **x Information Queries**
> **x Requests for Materials**

> _Requests for Services

Law Defines Terms? _Yes **x No**

When information contained in library records may be released:

> _With user consent
> [Consent must be in writing _Yes _No _Unclear]
> _Parent or guardian of minor seeks records of that minor
> _For library operation
> _Pursuant to a court order or subpoena
> _State Library request
> _Education Department Request

Remarks: The bill that amends the state of Idaho's public records act to exempt library records does not specify which libraries are covered and does not contain definitions. However, public libraries and libraries in public institutions would be covered and other types may be as well, depending on the intent of the legislature. No exemptions are given in the bill. Therefore, the public records act itself must be examined for this type of information.

Text of Law:

9-340 Records exempt from disclosure. The following records are exempt from disclosure:

(9) The records of a library which, when examined alone, or when examined with other public records, would reveal the identity of the library patron checking out, requesting, or using an item from a library.

Illinois   **Year of Passage: 1983**

Type of Law:

　　　　__Part of state records access law
　　　　x Separate law specific to libraries
　　　　__No law on confidentiality of library records

Types of Libraries covered:

　　　　x Public Libraries
　　　　x Public Academic
　　　　x Public Schools
　　　　__Library Systems
　　　　__Private Libraries open to the public
　　　　__Any library using public funds

Covered Records:

　　　　x Patron Registration
　　　　x Circulation Records
　　　　__Use of Materials in Library
　　　　__Information Queries
　　　　__Requests for Materials
　　　　__Requests for Services

Law Defines Terms? **x Yes** __No

When information contained in library records may be released:

    __With user consent
    [Consent must be in writing __Yes __No __Unclear]
    __Parent or guardian of minor seeks records of that minor
    __For library operation
    x Pursuant to a court order or subpoena
    __State Library request
    __Education Department Request

Remarks: The law includes public libraries and also the libraries of "educational, historical or eleemosynary" institutions, organizations or societies.

Text of Law:

PUBLIC ACT 83-179.

LOCAL LIBRARY ACT/PUBLIC LIBRARY DISTRICT ACT - SUBJECT TO LIBRARY RECORDS CONFIDENTIALITY ACT.

(House Bill No. 1669. Approved August 30, 1983.)

PUBLIC ACT TEXT

AN ACT regarding the confidentiality of various types of information held by certain libraries.

Be it enacted by the People of the State of Illinois, represented in the General Assembly:

(Ch.81, new par. 1201)

Section 1. (a) The registration and circulation records of a library are confidential information. Except pursuant to a court order, no person shall publish or make any information contained in such records available to the public.

(b) This Section does not prevent a library from publishing or making available to the public reasonable statistical reports regarding library registration and book circulation where those records are presented so that no individual is identified therein.

(c) For the purpose of this Section, (i) "library" means any public library or library or an educational, historical or eleemosynary institution, organization or society; (ii) "registration record" includes any information a library requires a person to provide in order for that person to become eligible to borrow books and other materials and (iii) "circulation records" includes all information identifying the individual borrowing particular books or materials.

(Ch. 81, new par. 1202)

Sec. 2. This Act shall be known and may be cited as The Library Records Confidentiality Act.

Section 3. Section 1-7 is added to "The Illinois Local Library Act," approved July 12, 1965, as amended, the added Section to read as follows:

(Ch. 81, new par. 1001-11)

Sec. 1-11. Each library subject to this Act is subject to the provisions of The Library Records Confidentiality Act.

PUBLIC ACT HISTORY

Passed in the General Assembly June 25, 1983.

Approved August 30, 1983.

Effective January 1, 1984.

Indiana   Year of Passage: 1980

Type of Law:

    x Part of state records access law
    __Separate law specific to libraries
    __No law on confidentiality of library records

Types of Libraries covered:

    x Public Libraries
    x Public Academic
    x Public Schools
    __Library Systems
    __Private Libraries open to the public
    __Any library using public funds

Covered Records:

    x Patron Registration
    x Circulation Records
    x Use of Materials in Library
    x Information Queries
    x Requests for Materials

_Requests for Services

Law Defines Terms? _Yes x No

When information contained in library records may be released:

_With user consent
[Consent must be in writing _Yes _No _Unclear]
_Parent or guardian of minor seeks records of that minor
_For library operation
x Pursuant to a court order or subpoena
_State Library request
_Education Department Request

Remarks: While the law does not state which specifically which types of libraries are covered, because it is part of the public records law, one can presume that public libraries and libraries at public institutions come under the law. Other types of libraries may, depending on the intent of the legislature.

Text of Law:

P.L. 34-1984

SECTION 2. IC 5-14-3-4, as amended by P.L.57-1983, Section 1, is amended to read as follows: Sec. 4. (a) The following public records are excepted from section 3 of this chapter and may not be disclosed by a public agency, unless access to the records is specifically required by a state or federal statute or is ordered by a court under the rules of discovery:

. . .

(16) Library records which can be used to identify any library patron.

Iowa   **Year of Passage: 1980**

Type of Law:

x Part of state records access law
_Separate law specific to libraries

_No law on confidentiality of library records

Types of Libraries covered:

> **x Public Libraries**
> _Public Academic
> _Public Schools
> _Library Systems
> _Private Libraries open to the public
> _Any library using public funds

Covered Records:

> **x Patron Registration**
> **x Circulation Records**
> **x Use of Materials in Library**
> **x Information Queries**
> **x Requests for Materials**
> _Requests for Services

Law Defines Terms? Yes **No**

When information contained in library records may be released:

> _With user consent
> [Consent must be in writing_Yes _No _Unclear]
> _Parent or guardian of minor seeks records of that minor
> _For library operation
> **x Pursuant to a court order or subpoena**
> _State Library request
> _Education Department Request

Text of Law:

CHAPTER 1024

LIBRARY RECORDS

H.F. 2240

AN ACT relating to the confidentiality of certain library records.

Be It Enacted by the General Assembly of the State of Iowa:

Section 1. Section sixty-eight A point seven (68A.7), Code 1979, is amended by adding the following new subsection:

NEW SUBSECTION. The records of a library which, by themselves or when examined with other public records, would reveal the identity of the library patron checking out or requesting an item from the library.

Section 2. This Act, being deemed of immediate importance, takes effect from and after its publication in The Waterloo Courier, a newspaper published in Waterloo, Iowa, and in the Atlantic-News Telegraph, a newspaper published in Atlantic, Iowa.

Approved March 21, 1980

I hereby certify that the foregoing Act, House File 2240, was published in The Waterloo Courier, Waterloo, Iowa on March 26, 1980, and in the Atlantic News-Telegraph, Atlantic, Iowa on March 25, 1980.

MELVIN D. SYNHORST, Secretary of State

Kansas   **Year of Passage: 1984**

Type of Law:

> x Part of state records access law
> _Separate law specific to libraries
> _No law on confidentiality of library records

Types of Libraries covered:

> x Public Libraries
> _Public Academic
> _Public Schools
> _Library Systems
> _Private Libraries open to the public
> _Any library using public funds

Covered Records:

> x Patron Registration
> x Circulation Records
> x Use of Materials in Library

    _Information Queries
    _Requests for Materials
    _Requests for Services

Law Defines Terms? Yes **No**

When information contained in library records may be released:

    _With user consent
      [Consent must be in writing_Yes _No _Unclear]
    _Parent or guardian of minor seeks records of that minor
    _For library operation
    _Pursuant to a court order or subpoena
    _State Library request
    _Education Department Request

Text of Law:

LAWS, JOURNALS AND PUBLIC INFORMATION

CHAPTER 187

House Bill No. 2668

(Amended by Chapter 282)

AN ACT concerning public records;

Be it enacted by the Legislature of the State of Kansas:

New Sec. 7. (a) Except to the extent disclosure is otherwise required by law, a public agency shall not be required to disclose:

. . . .

(23) Library patron and circulation records which pertain to identifiable individuals.

Kentucky

Kentucky has no law exempting library records from public inspection. However, there are Attorney General opinions exempting public and university library records from disclosure. Under Kentucky's Open Records statutes, Attorney General opinions have the force of law.

Louisiana   **Year of Passage: 1983**

Type of Law:

      _Part of state records access law
      x Separate law specific to libraries
      _No law on confidentiality of library records

Types of Libraries covered:

      _Public Libraries
      _Public Academic
      _Public Schools
      _Library Systems
      _Private Libraries open to the public
      x Any library using public funds

Covered Records:

      x Patron Registration
      x Circulation Records
      x Use of Materials in Library
      _Information Queries
      _Requests for Materials
      _Requests for Services

Law Defines Terms? _Yes **x No**

When information contained in library records may be released:

      x With user consent
        [Consent must be in writing **x Yes** _No _Unclear]
      x Parent or guardian of minor seeks records of
        that minor
      x For library operation
      x Pursuant to a court order or subpoena

__State Library request
__Education Department Request

Text of Law:

ACT No. 523

House Bill No. 962   BY: Miss Landrieu

AN ACT

To enact R.S. 44:13 to provide for the confidentiality of library registration and circulation records, and otherwise to provide with respect thereto.

Be it enacted by the Legislature of Louisiana:

Section 1. R.S. 44:13 is hereby enacted to read as follows:

§13. Registration records and other records of use maintained by libraries

A. Notwithstanding any provisions of this Chapter or any other law to the contrary, records of any library which is in whole or in part supported by public funds, including the records of public, academic, school, and special libraries, and the Louisiana State Library, indicating which of its documents or other materials, regardless of format, have been loaned or used by an identifiable individual or group of individuals may not be disclosed except to a parent or custodian of a minor child seeking access to that child's records, to persons acting within the scope of their duties in the administration of the library, to persons authorized in writing by the individual or group of individuals to inspect such records, of by order of a court of law.

B. Notwithstanding any provisions of this Chapter or any other law to the contrary, records of any such library which are maintained for purposes of registration or for determining eligibility for the use of library services may not be disclosed except as provided in Subsection A of this Section.

C. No provision of this Section shall be so construed as to prohibit or hinder any library or any business office operating jointly with a library from collecting overdue books, documents, films, or other items and/or materials owned or otherwise belonging to such library, nor shall any provision of this Section be so construed as to prohibit or hinder any such library or business office from collecting fines on such overdue books, documents, films, or other items and/or materials.

Approved by the Governor: July 8, 1983.

Published in the Official Journal of the State: July 27, 1983.

A true copy:

James H. "Jim" Brown

Secretary of State

Maine   **Year of Passage: 1983**

Type of Law:

      _Part of state records access law
      x Separate law specific to libraries
      _No law on confidentiality of library records

Types of Libraries covered:

      x Public Libraries
      _Public Academic
      _Public Schools
      _Library Systems
      _Private Libraries open to the public
      _Any library using public funds

Covered Records:

      _Patron Registration
      _Circulation Records
      _Use of Materials in Library
      _Information Queries
      _Requests for Materials
      _Requests for Services

Law Defines Terms? _Yes _No

When information contained in library records may be released:

      x With user consent
        [Consent must be in writing **x Yes** _No _Unclear]
      _Parent or guardian of minor seeks records of that minor
      _For library operation
      x Pursuant to a court order or subpoena

_State Library request
_Education Department Request

Remarks: The law says that "Records maintained by any public municipal library, including the Maine State Library" are those covered by the bill as passed. It also gives public municipal libraries up to 5 years from the law's effective date to comply.

Text of Law:

Chapter 208

S.P. 472 - L.D. 1436

AN ACT to Provide Confidentiality of Library Records

Be it enacted by the People of the State of Maine as follows

27 MRSA c. 4-A is enacted to read:

CHAPTER 4-A

LIBRARY RECORDS

§121. Confidentiality of library records

Records maintained by any public municipal library, including the Maine State Library, which contain information relating to the identity of a library patron relative to the patron's use of books or other materials at the library, shall be confidential. Those records may only be released with the express written permission of the patron involved or as the result of a court order.

Public municipal libraries shall have up to 5 years from the effective date of this chapter to be in compliance with this section.

Maryland   **Year of Passage: 1988**

Type of Law:

       _Part of state records access law
       x Separate law specific to libraries
       _No law on confidentiality of library records

Types of Libraries covered:

> **x Public Libraries**
> **x Public Academic**
> **x Public Schools**
> _Library Systems
> _Private Libraries open to the public
> _Any library using public funds

Covered Records:

> **x Patron Registration**
> **x Circulation Records**
> **x Use of Materials in Library**
> **x Information Queries**
> **x Requests for Materials**
> **x Requests for Services**

Law Defines Terms? _Yes **x No**

When information contained in library records may be released:

> _With user consent
> [Consent must be in writing _Yes _No _Unclear]
> _Parent or guardian of minor seeks records of that minor
> _For library operation
> _Pursuant to a court order or subpoena
> _State Library request
> _Education Department Request

Remarks: There are no specific exemptions allowing access to library records within the bill itself. There is, instead, the phrase, under 10-616(a), "Unless otherwise provided by law, a custodian shall deny inspection of a public record, as provided in this section." Therefore, it appears that the public records law itself must be examined for exemptions.

Text of Law:

1988

CHAPTER 233

(House Bill 1239)

AN ACT concerning

Libraries—Confidentially of Circulation Records

FOR the purpose of establishing the confidentiality of certain circulation records of certain libraries.

BY adding to

Article—Education

Section 23-107

Annotated Code of Maryland

(1985 Replacement Volume and 1987 Supplement)

BY repealing and reenacting, without amendments,

Article—State Government

Section 10-616(a) and (e)

Annotated Code of Maryland

(1984 Volume and 1987 Supplement)

BY repealing and reenacting, with amendments,

Article—State Government

Section 10-616(e)

Annotated Code of Maryland

(1984 Volume and 1987 Supplement)

SECTION 1. BE IT ENACTED BY THE GENERAL ASSEMBLY OF MARYLAND, That the Laws of Maryland read as follows:

Article - Education

23-107.

A FREE ASSOCIATION, SCHOOL, COLLEGE OR UNIVERSITY LIBRARY IN THIS STATE SHALL DENY INSPECTION OF A *ANY CIRCULATION RECORD OR OTHER ITEM, COLLECTION, OR GROUPING OF INFORMATION ABOUT AN INDIVIDUAL THAT:*

(1) IS MAINTAINED BY A LIBRARY;

(2) CONTAINS AN INDIVIDUAL'S NAME OR THE IDENTIFYING NUMBER, SYMBOL, OR OTHER IDENTIFYING PARTICULAR ASSIGNED TO THE INDIVIDUAL; AND

(3) IDENTIFIES THE USE A PATRON MAKES OF THAT LI-

BRARY'S MATERIALS, SERVICES, OR FACILITIES. THAT IDEN-
TIFIES THE TRANSACTIONS OF A BORROWER.

Article—State Government

10-616.

(a) Unless otherwise provided by law, a custodian shall deny inspection of a public record, as provided in this section.

(b) A custodian shall deny inspection of a circulation record of a public
library that identifies the transactions of borrower *OR OTHER
ITEM, COLLECTION, OR GROUPING OF INFORMATION ABOUT
AN INDIVIDUAL THAT:*

(1) IS MAINTAINED BY A LIBRARY;

*(2) CONTAINS AN INDIVIDUAL'S NAME OR THE IDENTIFYING
NUMBER, SYMBOL, OR OTHER IDENTIFYING PARTICULAR
ASSIGNED TO THE INDIVIDUAL; AND*

*(3) IDENTIFIES THE USE A PATRON MAKES OF THAT LI-
BRARY'S MATERIALS, SERVICES, OR FACILITIES.*

SECTION 2. AND BE IT FURTHER ENACTED, That this Act shall
take effect July 1, 1988.

Approved May 2, 1988.

Massachusetts   **Year of Passage: 1988**

Type of Law:

> **x Part of state records access law**
> __Separate law specific to libraries
> __No law on confidentiality of library records

Types of Libraries covered:

> **x Public Libraries**
> __Public Academic
> __Public Schools
> __Library Systems
> __Private Libraries open to the public
> __Any library using public funds

Covered Records:

>**x Patron Registration**
>**x Circulation Records**
>_Use of Materials in Library
>_Information Queries
>_Requests for Materials
>_Requests for Services

Law Defines Terms? _Yes **x No**

When information contained in library records may be released:

>_With user consent
>　[Consent must be in writing _Yes _No _Unclear]
>_Parent or guardian of minor seeks records of that minor
>_For library operation
>_Pursuant to a court order or subpoena
>_State Library request
>_Education Department Request

Remarks: The bill amending the Massachusetts public records act to provide confidentiality of library records does not in itself contain exemptions to the law. Therefore, the public records act must be examined to determine what exemptions exist under what conditions.

Text of Law:

Approved July 25, 1988

ACTS, 1988.—Chaps. 180, 181

Chapter 180. AN ACT FURTHER REGULATING THE DISCLO-SURE OF PUBLIC RECORDS.

Be it enacted, etc., as follows:

SECTION 1. Clause Twenty-sixth of section 7 of chapter 4 of the General Laws, as appearing in the 1986 Official Edition, is hereby amended by striking out subclause (k).

SECTION 2. Section 7 of chapter 78 of the General Laws, as so appearing, is hereby amended by adding the following two sentences:—That part of the records of a public library which reveals the identity and intellectual pursuits of a person using such library shall not be a public record as defined by clause Twenty-sixth of section seven of chapter four. Library authorities may disclose or exchange information relating to library users for the purposes of inter-library cooperation and coordination, including but not limited to, the purposes of facilitating the sharing of resources among library jurisdictions as authorized by clause (1) of section nineteen E or enforcing the provisions of sections ninety-nine and one hundred of chapter two hundred and sixty-six.

Approved July 25, 1988.

Michigan   **Year of Passage: 1982**

Type of Law:

     _Part of state records access law
     x Separate law specific to libraries
     _No law on confidentiality of library records

Types of Libraries covered:

     x Public Libraries
     x Public Academic
     x Public Schools
     x Library Systems
     x Private Libraries open to the public
     x Any library using public funds

Covered Records:

     x Patron Registration
     x Circulation Records
     x Use of Materials in Library
     _Information Queries
     x Requests for Materials
     _Requests for Services

Law Defines Terms? **Yes** No

When information contained in library records may be released:

     x With user consent

[Consent must be in writing **x Yes** __No __Unclear]
__Parent or guardian of minor seeks records of that minor
__For library operation
x Pursuant to a court order or subpoena
__State Library request
__Education Department Request

Text of Law:

[No. 455]

(HB 5066)

AN ACT to provide for the confidentiality of certain library records; and to provide for the selection and use of library materials.

The People of the State of Michigan enact:

397.601 Short title. [M.S.A. 15.1795(1)]

Sec. 1. This act shall be known and may be cited as "the library privacy act".

397.602 Definitions. [M.S.A. 15.1795(2)]

Sec. 2. As used in this act:

(a) "Library" includes a library which is established by the state; a county, city township, village, school district, or other local unit of government or authority or combination of local units of governments and authorities; a community college district; a college or university; or any private library open to the public.

(b) "Library record" means a document, record, or other method of storing information retained by a library that identifies a person as having requested or obtained specific materials from a library. Library record does not include nonidentifying material that may be retained for the purpose of studying or evaluating the circulation of library materials in general.

397.603 library record not subject to disclosure requirements; release or disclosure of library record without consent prohibited; exception; procedure and form of written consent; hearing. [M.S.A. 15.1795(3)]

Sec. 3. (1) A library record shall not be subject to the disclosure requirements of Act No. 442 of the Public Acts of 1976, as amended, being sections 15.231 to 15.246 of the Michigan Compiled Laws.

(2) Unless ordered by a court after giving the affected library notice of

the request and an opportunity to be heard thereon, a library or an employee or agent of a library shall not release or disclose a library record or portion of a library record to any person without the written consent of the person identified in that record. The procedure and form of giving written consent may be determined by the library.

(3a) At a hearing conducted pursuant to subsection (2), a library may appear and be represented by counsel.

397.604 Violation of §397.603; liability; civil action; damages; attorney fees and costs. [M.S.A. 15.1795(4)]

Sec. 4. A library or an agent or employee of a library which violates section 3 shall be liable to the person identified in a record that is improperly released or disclosed. The person identified may bring a civil action for actual damages or $250.00. whichever is greater; reasonable attorney fees; and the costs of bringing the action.

397.605 Selection and use of library materials. [M.S.A. 15.1795(5)]

Sec. 5. (1) Except as otherwise provided by statute or by a regulation adopted by the governing body of the library, the selection of library materials for inclusion in a library's collection shall be determined only by an employee of the library.

(2) Except as otherwise provided by law or by a regulation adopted by the governing body of the library, the use of library materials shall be determined only by an employee of the library.

Approved December 30, 1982.

Minnesota   **Year of Passage: 1982**

Type of Law:

      x Part of state records access law
      __Separate law specific to libraries
      __No law on confidentiality of library records

Types of Libraries covered:

      x Public Libraries
      x Public Academic
      x Public Schools

    x Library Systems
    __Private Libraries open to the public
    __Any library using public funds

Covered Records:

    x Patron Registration
    x Circulation Records
    x Use of Materials in Library
    x Information Queries
    x Requests for Materials
    __Requests for Services

Law Defines Terms? __Yes **x No**

When information contained in library records may be released:

    __With user consent
    [Consent must be in writing __Yes __No __Unclear]
    __Parent or guardian of minor seeks records of that minor
    __For library operation
    x Pursuant to a court order or subpoena
    __State Library request
    __Education Department Request

Text of Law:

13.40 Library Data

Subdivision 1. All records collected, maintained, used or disseminated by a library operated by any state agency, political subdivision or statewide system shall be administered in accordance with the provisions of this chapter.

Subd. 2. That portion of records maintained by a library which links a library patron's name with materials requested or borrowed by the patron or which links a patron's name with a specific subject about which the patron has requested information or materials is classified as private, pursuant to section 13.02, subdivision 132, and shall not be disclosed except pursuant to a valid court order.

Derivation:

Laws 1982, c. 545, Sections 6, 24.

Laws 1981, c. 311, Section 39.

Mississippi   **Year of Passage: 1992**

Type of Law:

      __Part of state records access law
      x Separate law specific to libraries
      __No law on confidentiality of library records

Types of Libraries covered:

      __Public Libraries
      __Public Academic
      __Public Schools
      __Library Systems
      __Private Libraries open to the public
      x Any library using public funds

Covered Records:

      x Patron Registration
      x Circulation Records
      x Use of Materials in Library
      __Information Queries
      __Requests for Materials
      __Requests for Services

Law Defines Terms? __Yes **x No**

When information contained in library records may be released:

      x With user consent
      [Consent must be in writing **x Yes** __No __Unclear]
      __Parent or guardian of minor seeks records of that minor
      __For library operation
      x Pursuant to a court order or subpoena
      __State Library request
      __Education Department Request

Text of Law:

SENATE BILL NO. 2065

AN ACT TO CREATE SECTION 39-3-365, MISSISSIPPI CODE OF

1972, TO PROVIDE FOR THE CONFIDENTIALITY OF CERTAIN LIBRARY RECORDS; AND FOR RELATED PURPOSES.

BE IT ENACTED BY THE LEGISLATURE OF THE STATE OF MISSISSIPPI:

SECTION 1. The following shall be codified as Section 39-3-365, Mississippi Code of 1972:

39-3-365. Records maintained by any library funded in whole or in part by public funds, which contain information relating to the identity of a library user, relative to the user's use of books or other materials at the library, shall be confidential. Such records may only be released with the express written permission of the respective library user or as the result of a court order.

SECTION 2. Aggregate statistics shown from registration and circulation records, with all personal identification removed, may be released or used by a library for research, planning and reporting purposes.

SECTION 3. No provision of this act shall be construed to prohibit any library, or any business operating jointly with a library, from disclosing information for the purpose of collecting overdue books, documents, films or other items or materials owned or otherwise belonging to such library. No provision of this act shall be construed to prohibit or hinder any such library or business office from collecting fines on such overdue books, documents, films or other items or materials.

SECTION 4. This act shall take effect and be in force from and after July 1, 1992.

** S.B. No. 2065   ST: Provide confidentiality for certain library records.

S06.S92R226. ASG

Missouri   **Year of Passage: 1986**

Type of Law:

    __Part of state records access law
    x Separate law specific to libraries
    __No law on confidentiality of library records

Types of Libraries covered:

x Public Libraries
x Public Academic
x Public Schools
__Library Systems
x Private Libraries open to the public
__Any library using public funds

Covered Records:

x Patron Registration
x Circulation Records
x Use of Materials in Library
__Information Queries
x Requests for Materials
__Requests for Services

Law Defines Terms? **x Yes** __No

When information contained in library records may be released:

x With user consent
   [Consent must be in writing **x Yes** __No __Unclear]
__Parent or guardian of minor seeks records of that minor
__For library operation
x Pursuant to a court order or subpoena
__State Library request
__Education Department Request

Text of law:

[H.B. 1372]

EDUCATION AND LIBRARIES: Libraries

AN ACT to repeal section 182.050, RSMo 1978 and section 570.200 RSMo as enacted by House Committee Substitute for Senate Bill 450 of the Second Regular Session of the 83rd General Assembly and as signed into law on March 17, 1986, relating to libraries, and to enact in lieu thereof four new sections relating to the same subject.

SECTION

A. Enacting clause

182.050. County library boards—appointment, qualifications, removal, vacancies—nepotism prohibited.

SECTION

570.200. Definitions

1. Disclosure of library records. definitions.

2. Disclosure of library records not required—exceptions

Be it enacted by the General Assembly of the State of Missouri, as follows:

Section A. Enacting clause.—Section 182.050, RSMo 1978 and section 570.200 RSMo as enacted by House Committee Substitute for Senate Bill 450 of the Second Regular Session of the 83rd General Assembly and as signed into law on March 17, 1986, is repealed and four new sections enacted in lieu thereof, to be known as sections 182.050, 570.200, 1 and 2, to read as follows:

182.050. **County library boards—appointment, qualification, removal, vacancies—nepotism prohibited.**—For the purpose of carrying into effect sections 182.010 to 182.120, in case a county library district is established and a free county library authorized as provided in section 182.010, within sixty days after the establishment of the county library district, there shall be created a county library board of trustees, of five members, who shall be residents of the library district, none of which shall be elected county officials. The members shall be appointed by the county commission for terms of four years each, except that as to members of the first board, two shall be appointed for one year, and one each shall be appointed for two years, three years, and four years, respectively, from the first day of July following their appointment; and annually thereafter before the first day of July the county commission shall appoint successors. Vacancies in the board occasioned by removals, resignations, or otherwise shall be reported to the county commission and shall be filled in like manner as original appointments; except that if the vacancy is in an unexpired term, the appointment shall be made for only the unexpired portion of that term. No member of the board shall receive compensation as such. No person shall be employed by the board of library trustees or by the librarian who is related within the third degree by blood or by marriage to any trustee of the board.

570.200. Definitions.—1. As used in this act, unless the context clearly indicates otherwise, the following terms shall mean:

(1) "Library", any public library or any library of an educational, historical or eleemosynary institution, organization or society;

(2) "Library card", a card or other device utilized by a library for purposes of identifying a person authorized to borrow library materi-

al, subject to all limitations and conditions imposed on such borrowing by the library issuing or honoring such card;

(3) "Library material", any book, plate, picture, photograph, engraving, painting, sculpture, artifact, drawing, map, newspaper, microform, sound recording, audiovisual material, magnetic or other tape, electronic data processing record or other document, written or printed material, regardless of physical form or characteristic, which is a constituent element of a library's collection or any part thereof, belonging to, on loan to, or otherwise in the custody of a library;

(4) "Notice in writing", any notice deposited as certified or registered mail in the United States mail and addressed to the person at his address as it appears on the library card or to his last known address. The notice shall contain a statement that failure to return the library material within ten days of receipt of the notice may subject the user to criminal prosecution.

(5) "Premises of a library", a building structure or other enclosure in which a library is located or in which the library keeps, displays and makes available for inspection, borrowing or return of library materials.

Section 1. Disclosure of library records, definitions.—As used in sections 1 and 2 of this act, the following terms shall mean:

(1) "Library", any library established by the state or any political subdivision of the state, or combination thereof, by any community college district, or by any college or university, and any private library open to the public;

(2) "Library material", any book, document, film, record, art work, or other library property which a patron may use, borrow or request:

(3) "Library record", any document, record, or other method of storing information retained, received or generated by a library that identifies a person or persons as having requested, used, or borrowed library material, and all other records identifying the names of library users. The term "library records" does not include nonidentifying material that may be retained for the purpose of studying or evaluating the circulation of library material in general.

Section 2. Disclosure of library records not required—exceptions.—Notwithstanding the provisions of any other law to the contrary, no library or employee or agent of a library shall be required to release or disclose a library record or portion of a library to any person or persons except:

(1) In response to a written request of the person identified in that record, according to procedures and forms giving written consent as determined by the library; or

(2) In response to an order issued by a court of competent jurisdiction

upon a finding that the disclosure of such record is necessary to protect the public safety or to prosecute a crime.

Approved June 19, 1986.

Montana   **Year of Passage: 1985**

Type of Law:

    __Part of state records access law
    x Separate law specific to libraries
    __No law on confidentiality of library records

Types of Libraries covered:

    x Public Libraries
    x Public Academic
    x Public Schools
    __Library Systems
    x Private Libraries open to the public
    __Any library using public funds

Covered Records:

    x Patron Registration
    x Circulation Records
    x Use of Materials in Library
    __Information Queries
    x Requests for Materials
    __Requests for Services

Law Defines Terms? **x Yes** __No

When information contained in library records may be released:

    x With user consent
    [Consent must be in writing **x Yes** __No __Unclear]
    __Parent or guardian of minor seeks records of that minor
    x For library operation
    x Pursuant to a court order or subpoena

_State Library request
_Education Department Request

Text of Law:

Library Records Confidentiality Act

22-1-1101. Short title. This part may be cited as the "Montana Library Records Confidentiality Act."

22-1-1102. Definitions. As used in 22-1-1103, the following definitions apply:

(1) "Library" means a library that is established by the state, a county, city, town, school district, or a combination of those units of government, a college or university, or any private library open to the public.

(2) "Library records" means any document, record, or any other method of storing information retained, received, or generated by a library that identifies a person as having requested, used, or borrowed library material or other records identifying the names or other personal identifiers of library users. Library records does not include nonidentifying material that may be retained for the purpose of studying or evaluating the circulation of library materials in general or records that are not retained or retrieved by personal identifier.

22-1-1103. Nondisclosure of library records. (1) No person may release or disclose a library record or portion of a library record to any person except in response to:

(a) a written request of the person identified in that record, according to procedures and forms giving written consent as determined by the library; or

(b) an order issued by a court of competent jurisdiction, upon a finding that the disclosure of such record is necessary because the merits of public disclosure clearly exceed the demand for individual privacy.

(2) A library is not prevented from publishing or making available to the public reasonable statistical reports regarding library registration and book circulation if those reports are presented so that no individual is identified therein.

(3) Library records may be disclosed to the extent necessary to return overdue or stolen materials or collect fines.

22-1-1104 through 22-1-1110 reserved.

22-1-1111. Penalty. Any person who violates 22-1-1103 is guilty of a misdemeanor and is liable to the person identified in a record that is improperly released or disclosed. The person identified may bring a civil action for actual damages or $100, whichever is greater. Reasonable attorney fees and the costs of bringing the action may be awarded to the prevailing party.

Nebraska   **Year of Passage: 1983**

Type of Law:

> **x Part of state records access law**
> __Separate law specific to libraries
> __No law on confidentiality of library records

Types of Libraries covered:

> __Public Libraries
> __Public Academic
> __Public Schools
> __Library Systems
> __Private Libraries open to the public
> **x Any library using public funds**

Covered Records:

> **x Patron Registration**
> **x Circulation Records**
> **x Use of Materials in Library**
> **x Information Queries**
> **x Requests for Materials**
> **x Requests for Services**

Law Defines Terms? __Yes **x No**

When information contained in library records may be released:

> __With user consent
> [Consent must be in writing __Yes __No __Unclear]
> __Parent or guardian of minor seeks records of that minor
> __For library operation
> __Pursuant to a court order or subpoena

__State Library request
__Education Department Request

Remarks: Records may be withheld "unless publicly disclosed in an open court, open administrative proceeding, or open meeting, or disclosed by a public entity pursuant to its duties."

Text of Law:

CHAPTER 84 STATE OFFICERS

ARTICLE 7 GENERAL PROVISIONS AS TO STATE OFFICERS

84-712.05 Records which may be withheld from the public enumerated:

The following records, unless publicly disclosed in an open court, open administrative proceeding, or open meeting, or disclosed by a public entity pursuant to its duties, may be withheld from the public by the lawful custodian of the records:

. . .

(10) Records or portions of records kept by a publicly funded library which when examined with or without other records, reveal the identity of any library patron using the library's materials or services;. . .

Nevada   **Year of Passage: 1981**

Type of Law:

> **x Part of state records access law**
> __Separate law specific to libraries
> __No law on confidentiality of library records

Types of Libraries covered:

> **x Public Libraries**
> __Public Academic
> __Public Schools
> __Library Systems

_Private Libraries open to the public
_Any library using public funds

Covered Records:

x Patron Registration
x Circulation Records
x Use of Materials in Library
_Information Queries
_Requests for Materials
_Requests for Services

Law Defines Terms? _Yes **x No**

When information contained in library records may be released:

_With user consent
  [Consent must be in writing _Yes _No _Unclear]
_Parent or guardian of minor seeks records of that minor
_For library operation
x Pursuant to a court order or subpoena
_State Library request
_Education Department Request

Text of Law:

Senate Bill No.25-Committee on Human Resources and Facilities

CHAPTER 84

AN ACT relating to records of libraries; providing that records of circulation are not public records; restricting disclosure of such records; and providing other matters properly relating thereto.

[Approved April 10, 1981]

The People of the State of Nevada, represented in Senate and Assembly, do enact as follows:

SECTION 1. Chapter 239 of NRS is hereby amended by adding thereto a new section which shall read as follows:

Any records of a public library or other library which contain the identity of a user and the books, documents, films, recordings or other property of the library which he used are confidential and not public books or records within the meaning of NRS 239.010. Such records my be disclosed only in response to an order issued by a court upon a finding that the disclosure of such records is necessary to protect the public safety or to prosecute a crime.

New Hampshire   **Year of Passage: 1989**

Type of Law:

    _Part of state records access law
    x Separate law specific to libraries
    _No law on confidentiality of library records

Types of Libraries covered:

    x Public Libraries
    x Public Academic
    x Public Schools
    x Library Systems
    x Private Libraries open to the public
    x Any library using public funds

Covered Records:

    x Patron Registration
    x Circulation Records
    x Use of Materials in Library
    x Information Queries
    x Requests for Materials
    x Requests for Services

Law Defines Terms? _Yes **x No**

When information contained in library records may be released:

    x With user consent
    [Consent must be in writing _Yes **x No** _Unclear]
    _Parent or guardian of minor seeks records of that minor
    x For library operation
    x Pursuant to a court order or subpoena
    _State Library request

__Education Department Request

Remarks: The New Hampshire law applies to users of "public or other than public libraries."

Text of Law:

CHAPTER 184 (H 36)
AN ACT RELATIVE TO LIBRARY RECORDS CONFIDENTIALITY.

Be it Enacted by the Senate and House of Representatives in General Court convened:

184:1 Purpose Statement. The Access to Public Records and Meetings Law, RSA 91-A, or Right-to-Know Law, does not include a definition of what constitutes a public record. The New Hampshire supreme court has applied a balancing test to determine whether a record is public by weighing the benefits of disclosure to the public versus the benefits of nondisclosure. By weighing the benefits of allowing disclosure of library user records against the benefits of denial of disclosure, the general court has determined that the benefits of nondisclosure clearly prevail. This act, therefore, exempts library user records from RSA 91-A to ensure that the individual's right to privacy regarding the nature of the library materials used by the individual is not invaded. To protect the privacy of all New Hampshire citizens, both public and other than public library records are protected.

184:2 Library User Records Exempt. Amend RSA 91-A:5, IV to read as follows:

IV. Records pertaining to internal personnel practices; confidential, commercial, or financial information; test questions, scoring keys, and other examination data used to administer a licensing examination, examination for employment, or academic examinations; and personnel, medical, welfare, library user, and other files whose disclosure would constitute invasion of privacy. Without otherwise compromising the confidentiality of the files, nothing in this paragraph shall prohibit a body or agency from releasing information relative to health or safety from investigative files on a limited basis to persons whose health or safety may be affected.

184.3 New Section; Confidential Library User Records. Amend RSA 201-D by inserting after section 10 the following new section:

201-D:11 Library User Records; Confidentiality.

I. Library records which contain the names or other personal identifying information regarding the users of public or other than public libraries shall be confidential and shall not be disclosed except as provided in paragraph II. Such records include, but are not limited to, library, information system, and archival records related to the circulation and use of library materials or services.

II. Records described in paragraph I may be disclosed to the extent necessary for the proper operation of such libraries and shall be disclosed upon request by or consent of the user or pursuant to subpoena, court order, or where otherwise required by statute.

III. Nothing in this section shall be construed to prohibit any library from releasing statistical information and other data regarding the circulation or use of library materials, provided, however, that the identity of the users of such library materials shall be considered confidential and shall not be disclosed to the general public except as provided in paragraph II.

184:4 Effective Date. This act shall take effect 60 days after its passage.

[Approved May 22, 1989.]

[Effective Date July 21, 1989.]

New Jersey   **Year of Passage: 1985**

Type of Law:

    __Part of state records access law
    x Separate law specific to libraries
    __No law on confidentiality of library records

Types of Libraries covered:

    x Public Libraries
    x Public Academic
    x Public Schools
    x Library Systems
    x Private Libraries open to the public
    x Any library using public funds

Covered Records:

    x Patron Registration

x Circulation Records
__Use of Materials in Library
__Information Queries
__Requests for Materials
__Requests for Services

Law Defines Terms? **x Yes** __No

When information contained in library records may be released:

x With user consent
  [Consent must be in writing __Yes **x No** __Unclear]
__Parent or guardian of minor seeks records of that minor
x For library operation
x Pursuant to a court order or subpoena
__State Library request
__Education Department Request

Text of Law:

CHAPTER 172

AN ACT concerning library records and supplementing chapter 73 of Title 18A of the New Jersey Statutes.

BE IT ENACTED *by the Senate and General Assembly of the State of New Jersey:*

C. 18A:73-43.1 "Library," "library record" defined.

1. For the purposes of this act:

a. "Library" means a library maintained by any State or local governmental agency, school, college, or industrial, commercial or other special group, association or agency, whether public or private.

b. "Library record" means any document or record, however maintained, the primary purpose of which is to provide for control of the circulation or other public use of library materials.

C. 18A:73-43.2 confidentiality; exceptions.

2. Library records which contain the names or other personally identifying details regarding the users of libraries are confidential and shall not be disclosed except in the following circumstances:

a. The records are necessary for the proper operation of the library;

b. Disclosure is requested by the user; or

c. Disclosure is required pursuant to a subpoena issued by a court or court order.

C. 18A:73-43.3 Rules, regulations.

3. The State Librarian shall adopt pursuant to section 18 of P.L. 1969, c. 158 (C. 18A:73-33)and the "Administrative Procedure Act," P.L. 1968, c. 410 (C. 52:14B-1 et seq.) rules and regulations necessary to effectuate the purposes of this act.

4. This act shall take effect immediately.

Approved May 31, 1985.

New Mexico   **Year of Passage: 1989**

Type of Law:

   __Part of state records access law
   x Separate law specific to libraries
   __No law on confidentiality of library records

Types of Libraries covered:

   x Public Libraries
   x Public Academic
   x Public Schools
   x Library Systems
   __Private Libraries open to the public
   x Any library using public funds

Covered Records:

   x Patron Registration
   x Circulation Records
   x Use of Materials in Library
   __Information Queries
   x Requests for Materials
   __Requests for Services

Law Defines Terms? **x Yes** __No

When information contained in library records may be released:

x With user consent
   [Consent must be in writing **x Yes** __No __Unclear]
x Parent or guardian of minor seeks records of that minor
   __For library operation
x Pursuant to a court order or subpoena
   __State Library request
   __Education Department Request

Remarks: The law requires that only school libraries release the records of minors to parents or guardians.

Text of Law:

Laws of 1989 Chapter 151   AN ACT

RELATING TO LIBRARIES; ENACTING THE LIBRARY PRIVACY ACT; PROTECTING THE CONFIDENTIALITY OF PERSONAL LIBRARY RECORDS.

BE IT ENACTED BY THE LEGISLATURE OF THE STATE OF NEW MEXICO:

Section 1. SHORT TITLE.—This act may be cited as the "Library Privacy Act."

Section 2. PURPOSE.—The purpose of the Library Privacy Act is to preserve the intellectual freedom guaranteed by Sections 4 and 17 of Article 2 of the constitution of New Mexico by providing privacy for users of the public libraries of the state with respect to the library materials that they wish to use.

Section 3. DEFINITIONS.—As used in the Library Privacy Act:

A. "library" includes any library receiving public funds, any library that is a state agency and any library established by the state, an instrumentality of the state, a local government, district or authority, whether or not that library is regularly open to the public; and

B. "patron record" means any document, record or other method of storing information retained by a library that identifies, or when combined with other available information identifies, a person as a patron of the library or that indicates use or request of materials from the library. "Patron record" includes patron registration information and circulation information that identifies specific patrons.

Section 4. RELEASE OF PATRON RECORDS PROHIBITED.—
Patron records shall not be disclosed or released to any person not a
member of the library staff in the performance of his duties, except
upon written consent of the person identified in the record, or except
upon court order issued to the library. The library shall have the right
to be represented by counsel at any hearing on disclosure or release of
its patron records.

Section 5. EXCEPTIONS.—The prohibition on the release or disclosure of patron records in Section 4 of the Library Privacy Act shall not
apply to overdue notices or to the release or disclosure by school
libraries to the legal guardian of the patron records of unemancipated
minors or legally incapacitated persons.

Section 6. VIOLATIONS—CIVIL LIABILITY.—Any person who
violates Section 4 of the Library Privacy Act shall be subject to civil
liability to the person identified in the released records for damages
and costs of the action as determined by the court.

Senate Bill 245, aa

Approved March 29, 1989

New York   **Year of Passage: 1981**

Type of Law:

    _Part of state records access law
    _Separate law specific to libraries
    _No law on confidentiality of library records

Types of Libraries covered:

    x Public Libraries
    x Public Academic
    x Public Schools
    x Library Systems
    x Private Libraries open to the public
    x Any library using public funds

Covered Records:

    x Patron Registration

x Circulation Records
__Use of Materials in Library
__Information Queries
__Requests for Materials
__Requests for Services

Law Defines Terms? __Yes **x** **No**

When information contained in library records may be released:

x With user consent
[Consent must be in writing **x Yes** __No __Unclear]
__Parent or guardian of minor seeks records of that minor
x For library operation
x Pursuant to a court order or subpoena
__State Library request
__Education Department Request

Remarks: The New York law is part of the state's civil practice law and rules.

Text of Law:

5953-B 1981-1982 Regular Sessions March 3, 1981 R.R. 222

Introduced by M. of A. Sanders—Multi-sponsored by—M. of A. Grannis, Hevesi, Nadler, Feldman—read once and referred to the Committee on Governmental Operations—reported and referred to the Committee on Rules—Rules committee discharged, bill amended, ordered reprinted as amended and recommitted to the Committee on Rules—amended on special order of third reading, ordered reprinted as amended, retaining its place on the special order of third reading.

AN ACT to amend the civil practice law and rules, in relation to library records.

The People of the State of New York, represented in Senate and Assembly, do enact as follows:

Section 1. The civil practice law and rules is amended by adding a new section forty-five hundred nine to read as follows:

S 4509. *Library circulation records. Records related to the circulation of library materials which contain names or other personally identifying details regarding the users of public, private, school, college and university libraries of this state shall be confidential and shall not be disclosed except that such records may be disclosed to the extent necessary for the proper operation of such library and shall be disclosed upon request or consent of the user or pursuant to subpoena, court order or where otherwise required by statute.*

S 2. This act shall take effect immediately.

Note: Underlined matter is new.

North Carolina   **Year of Passage: 1985**

Type of Law:

    __Part of state records access law
    x Separate law specific to libraries
    __No law on confidentiality of library records

Types of Libraries covered:

    x Public Libraries
    x Public Academic
    x Public Schools
    x Library Systems
    x Private Libraries open to the public
    x Any library using public funds

Covered Records:

    x Patron Registration
    x Circulation Records
    x Use of Materials in Library
    x Information Queries
    x Requests for Materials
    x Requests for Services

Law Defines Terms? **x Yes** __No

When information contained in library records may be released:

    x With user consent

[Consent must be in writing x Yes __No __Unclear]
__Parent or guardian of minor seeks records of that minor
x For library operation
x Pursuant to a court order or subpoena
__State Library request
__Education Department Request

Text of Law:

GENERAL ASSEMBLY OF NORTH CAROLINA

SESSION 1985

RATIFIED BILL

CHAPTER 486

HOUSE BILL 724

AN ACT RELATING TO CONFIDENTIALITY OF LIBRARY USER RECORDS.

The General Assembly of North Carolina enacts:

Section 1. This act may be cited as the Library Privacy Act.

Section 2. Chapter 125 of the General Statutes is amended by adding a new Article to read:

"Article 3.

"Library Records.

"Section 125-18. *Definitions.*—As used in this Article, unless the context requires otherwise:

(1) 'Library' means a library established by the State; a county, city, township, village, school district, or other local unit of government or authority or combination of local units of governments and authorities; a community college or university; or any private library open to the public.

(2) 'Library record' means a document, record, or other method of storing information retained by a library that identifies a person as having requested or obtained specific information or materials from a library. 'Library record' does not include nonidentifying material that may be retained for the purpose of studying or evaluating the circulation of library materials in general.

"Section 125-19. *Confidentiality of library user records.*—

(a) Disclosure. A library shall not disclose any library record that identifies a person as having requested or obtained specific materials, information, or services, or as otherwise having used the library, except as provided in the following instances:

(1) When necessary for the reasonable operation of the library;

(2) Upon written consent of the user; or

(3) Pursuant to subpoena, court order, or where otherwise required by law."

Section 3. This act shall become effective October 1, 1985.

In the General Assembly read three times and ratified, this the 27th day of June, 1985.

North Dakota   **Year of Passage: 1985**

Type of Law:

> **x Part of state records access law**
> _Separate law specific to libraries
> _No law on confidentiality of library records

Types of Libraries covered:

> _Public Libraries
> _Public Academic
> _Public Schools
> _Library Systems
> _Private Libraries open to the public
> **x Any library using public funds**

Covered Records:

> **x Patron Registration**
> **x Circulation Records**
> **x Use of Materials in Library**
> **x Information Queries**
> **x Requests for Materials**
> **x Requests for Services**

Law Defines Terms? __Yes x No

When information contained in library records may be released:

> __With user consent
> [Consent must be in writing __Yes __No __Unclear]
> __Parent or guardian of minor seeks records of that minor
> __For library operation
> **x Pursuant to a court order or subpoena**
> __State Library request
> __Education Department Request

Text of Law:

CHAPTER 464

HOUSE BILL NO. 1270

(Representative Unhjem)

(Senator Waldera)

LIBRARY RECORDS NOT OPEN RECORDS

AN ACT to create and enact a new section to chapter 40-38 of the North Dakota Century Code, relating to records maintained by public libraries.

BE IT ENACTED BY THE LEGISLATIVE ASSEMBLY OF THE STATE OF NORTH DAKOTA:

SECTION 1. A new section to chapter 40-38 of the North Dakota Century Code is hereby created and enacted to read as follows:

Library records—Open records exception. Any record maintained or received by a library receiving public funds, which provides a library patron's name or information sufficient to identify a patron together with the subject about which the patron requested information, is considered private and is excepted from the public records disclosure requirements of section 44-04-18. These records may be released when required pursuant to a court order or a subpoena.

Approved March 14, 1985

Ohio

Ohio does not have a law exempting library records from public inspection. However, library records are protected by limited confidentiality and administrative policy. Several times bills to exempt library records have died in committee.

Oklahoma   **Year of Passage: 1986**

Type of Law:

    __Part of state records access law
    x Separate law specific to libraries
    __No law on confidentiality of library records

Types of Libraries covered:

    __Public Libraries
    __Public Academic
    __Public Schools
    __Library Systems
    __Private Libraries open to the public
    x Any library using public funds

Covered Records:

    x Patron Registration
    x Circulation Records
    x Use of Materials in Library
    __Information Queries
    x Requests for Materials
    x Requests for Services

Law Defines Terms? __Yes **x No**

When information contained in library records may be released:

    x With user consent
      [Consent must be in writing **x Yes** __No __Unclear]
    __Parent or guardian of minor seeks records of that minor
    x For library operation
    x Pursuant to a court order or subpoena
    __State Library request

__Education Department Request

Remarks: A special section of the law allows middle and elementary school libraries to maintain records that identify individuals or groups to whom library materials have been loaned even if that system reveals who such persons or groups are.

Text of Law:

PUBLIC LIBRARIES—RECORD DISCLOSURE—EXCEPTIONS

CHAPTER 98

H.B. 1828

AN ACT RELATING TO PUBLIC LIBRARIES;AMENDING

SECTION 1, CHAPTER 81, O.S.L. 1985 (65 O.S. SUPP.

1985, SECTION 1-105), WHICH PROHIBITS DISCLOSURE OF CERTAIN

RECORDS BY CERTAIN LIBRARIES; PROVIDING

EXCEPTIONS; PERMITTING MAINTAINING OF CERTAIN

SYSTEMS OF RECORDS; AND PROVIDING AN EFFECTIVE DATE.

BE IT ENACTED BY THE PEOPLE OF THE STATE OF OKLAHOMA:

SECTION 1. AMENDATORY Section 1, Chapter 81, O.S.L. 1985 (65 O.S. Supp. 1985, Section 1-105), is amended to read as follows:

Section 1-105. A. Any library which is in whole or in part supported by public funds including but not limited to public, academic, school or special libraries, and having records indicating which of its documents or other materials, regardless of format, have been loaned to or used by an identifiable individual or group shall not disclose such records to any person except to:

1. Persons acting within the scope of their duties in the administration of the library;

2. Persons authorized to inspect such records, in writing, by the individual or group; or

3. By order of a court of law.

B. *The requirements of this section shall not prohibit middle and elementary school libraries from maintaining a system of records that identifies the individual or group to whom library materials have been loaned even if such system permits a determination, independent of any disclosure of such information to the library, that documents or materials have been loaned to an individual or group.*

Section 2. This act shall become effective November 1, 1986.

Approved April 5, 1986.

Note: Underlined material amends the earlier law, H.B. 1246, passed in May of 1985.

Oregon   **Year of Passage: 1983**

Type of Law:

    _Part of state records access law
    _Separate law specific to libraries
    _No law on confidentiality of library records

Types of Libraries covered:

    _Public Libraries
    _Public Academic
    _Public Schools
    _Library Systems
    _Private Libraries open to the public
    _Any library using public funds

Covered Records:

    _Patron Registration
    _Circulation Records
    _Use of Materials in Library
    _Information Queries
    _Requests for Materials
    _Requests for Services

Law Defines Terms? _Yes _No

When information contained in library records may be released:

    _With user consent

[Consent must be in writing _Yes _No _Unclear]
_Parent or guardian of minor seeks records of that minor
_For library operation
_Pursuant to a court order or subpoena
_State Library request
_Education Department Request

Text of Law:

SECTION 11. ORS 192.005 is amended to read:

. . .*

(5) "Public record" means a document, book, paper, photograph, file, sound recording or other material, such as court files, mortgage and deed records, regardless of physical form or characteristics, made, received, filed or recorded in pursuance of law or in connection with the transaction of public business, whether or not confidential or restricted in use. "Public records" includes correspondence, public records made by phototcopying and public writings, but does not include:

*. . .

(b) Library and museum materials made or acquired and preserved solely for reference or exhibition purposes.

*Parts of the law that were omitted because they were not relevant to the topic at hand.

Pennsylvania   **Year of Passage: 1984**

Type of Law:

       _Part of state records access law
       x Separate law specific to libraries
       _No law on confidentiality of library records

Types of Libraries covered:

       x Public Libraries
       x Public Academic
       x Public Schools

x Library Systems
_Private Libraries open to the public
_Any library using public funds

Covered Records:

x Patron Registration
x Circulation Records
_Use of Materials in Library
_Information Queries
_Requests for Materials
_Requests for Services

Law Defines Terms? _Yes **x No**

When information contained in library records may be released:

_With user consent
   [Consent must be in writing _Yes _No _Unclear]
_Parent or guardian of minor seeks records of that minor
_For library operation
x Pursuant to a court order or subpoena
_State Library request
_Education Department Request

Text of Law:

SESSION OF 1984 No. 1984-90

AN ACT

SB 658

Amending the act of June 14, 1961 (P.L. 324, No. 188), entitled

"An act relating to the establishment, operation and maintenance of the State Library and public libraries in the Commonwealth; amending, revising, consolidating and changing the laws relating thereto; imposing duties upon public officers; providing for State and local cooperation and assistance in the establishment and maintenance of libraries; prescribing penalties; and repealing existing laws," further providing for municipality powers to make appropriations and impose taxes to fund libraries; and providing for the confidentiality of library circulation records.

The General Assembly of the Commonwealth of Pennsylvania hereby enacts as follows:

. . . *

Section 3. The act is amended by adding a section to read:

Section 428. Library Circulation Records.—Records related to the circulation of library materials which contain the names or other personally identifying details regarding the users of the State Library or any local library which is established or maintained under any law of the Commonwealth or the library of any university, college or education institution chartered by the Commonwealth or the library of any public school or branch reading room, deposit station or agency operated in connection therewith, shall be confidential and shall not be made available to anyone except by a court order in a criminal proceeding.

Section 5. This act shall take effect immediately.

APPROVED—The 27th day of June, A.D. 1984.

DICK THORNBURGH

*Sections 1, 2, and 4 are not included here because they deal with other public library matters, not the confidentiality of library records.

Rhode Island   **Year of Passage: 1984**

Type of Law:

     x Part of state records access law
     _Separate law specific to libraries
     _No law on confidentiality of library records

Types of Libraries covered:

     _Public Libraries
     _Public Academic
     _Public Schools
     _Library Systems
     _Private Libraries open to the public
     _Any library using public funds

Covered Records:

     x Patron Registration

    x Circulation Records
    x Use of Materials in Library
    __Information Queries
    x Requests for Materials
    __Requests for Services

Law Defines Terms? x Yes __No

When information contained in library records may be released:

    __With user consent
      [Consent must be in writing __Yes __No __Unclear]
    __Parent or guardian of minor seeks records of that minor
    __For library operation
    __Pursuant to a court order or subpoena
    __State Library request
    __Education Department Request

Text of Law:

CHAPTER 372

84-H 7750A

Approved May 11, 1984

AN ACT RELATING TO OPEN MEETINGS AND PUBLIC RECORDS

It is enacted by the General Assembly as follows:

. . . *

38-2-2. Definitions.—As used in this chapter:

(b) "Public body" means any department, agency, commission, committee, board, council, bureau or authority or any subdivision thereof of state or municipal government. for purposes of this section, any political party, organization or unit thereof meeting or convening for any purpose, is not and should not be considered to be a public body.

. . .

(d)"Public record" or "public records" shall mean all documents, papers, letters, maps, books, tapes, photographs, films, sound recordings, or other material regardless of physical form or characteristics made or received pursuant to law or ordinance or in connection with the transaction of official business by any agency. For the purposes of this chapter, the following records shall not be deemed public:

. . .

(21)Library records which, by themselves, or when examined with other public records, would reveal the identity of the library user requesting, checking out, or using any library materials.

However, any reasonably segregable portion as determined by the chief administrative officer of the public body of a public record excluded by this section shall be available for public inspections after the deletion of the information which is the basis of the exclusion, if disclosure of said segregable portion does not violate the intent of this section.

(e) "Chief administrative officer" means the highest authority of the public body as defined in subsection (a) of this section.

*Sections of this bill which are not relevant to the confidentiality of library records have been omitted.

South Carolina   **Year of Passage: 1985**

Type of Law:

    _Part of state records access law
    x Separate law specific to libraries
    _No law on confidentiality of library records

Types of Libraries covered:

    _Public Libraries
    _Public Academic
    _Public Schools
    _Library Systems
    _Private Libraries open to the public
    x Any library using public funds

Covered Records:

    x Patron Registration
    x Circulation Records
    x Use of Materials in Library
    x Information Queries
    x Requests for Materials
    x Requests for Services

Law Defines Terms? x Yes __No

When information contained in library records may be released:

x With user consent
[Consent must be in writing __Yes x No __Unclear]
__Parent or guardian of minor seeks records of that minor
x For library operation
x Pursuant to a court order or subpoena
__State Library request
__Education Department Request

Remarks: The South Carolina law covers private, as well as public, libraries which receive or expend any public funds.

Text of Law:

No. 108

(R157, S229)

AN ACT TO AMEND TITLE 60, CODE OF LAWS OF SOUTH CAROLINA, 1976, RELATING TO LIBRARIES, ARCHIVES, MUSEUMS, AND ARTS, BY ADDING CHAPTER 4 SO AS TO PROVIDE THAT RECORDS RELATED TO REGISTRATION AND CIRCULATION OF LIBRARY MATERIALS WHICH CONTAIN NAMES OR OTHER PERSONALLY IDENTIFYING DETAILS REGARDING THE USERS OF PUBLIC, PRIVATE, SCHOOL, COLLEGE, TECHNICAL COLLEGE, UNIVERSITY, AND STATE INSTITUTIONAL LIBRARIES AND LIBRARY SYSTEMS, SUPPORTED IN WHOLE OR IN PART BY PUBLIC FUNDS OR EXPENDING PUBLIC FUNDS ARE CONFIDENTIAL INFORMATION; TO INCLUDE AS CONFIDENTIAL INFORMATION RECORDS WHICH REVEAL THE IDENTITY OF THE LIBRARY PATRON CHECKING OUT OR REQUESTING AN ITEM FROM THE LIBRARY OR USING OTHER LIBRARY SERVICES; TO EXCLUDE FROM CONFIDENTIAL RECORDS NONIDENTIFYING ADMINISTRATIVE AND STATISTICAL REPORTS OF REGISTRATION AND CIRCULATION; TO ALLOW FOR DISCLOSURE OF THE CONFIDENTIAL INFORMATION TO PERSONS ACTING WITHIN THE SCOPE OF THEIR DUTIES IN THE ADMINISTRATION OF THE LIBRARY OR LIBRARY SYSTEM OR PERSONS AUTHORIZED BY THE LIBRARY PATRON TO INSPECT HIS RECORDS, OR IN ACCORDANCE WITH PROPER JUDICIAL ORDER IF THE DISCLOSURE IS NECESSARY TO PROTECT PUBLIC SAFETY, TO PROSECUTE A CRIME, OR UPON SHOWING OF GOOD CAUSE BEFORE THE PRESIDING JUDGE IN A CIVIL MATTER; TO DEFINE "REGIS-

TRATION RECORDS" AND "CIRCULATION RECORDS"; AND TO PROVIDE PENALTIES FOR VIOLATIONS; AND TO AMEND SECTION 30-1-10, RELATING TO PUBLIC RECORDS, REPORTS, AND OFFICIAL DOCUMENTS, AND ACT 593 OF 1978, AS AMENDED, RELATING TO THE FREEDOM OF INFORMATION ACT, SO AS TO EXCLUDE FROM THE DEFINITION OF "PUBLIC RECORDS" THE RECORDS IDENTIFIED IN CHAPTER 4 OF TITLE 60 AS CONFIDENTIAL INFORMATION.

Be it enacted by the General Assembly of the State of South Carolina:

Confidential library records

SECTION 1. Title 60 of the 1976 Code is amended by adding:

"CHAPTER 4

Confidential Library Records

Section 60-4-10. Records related to registration and circulation of library materials which contain names or other personally identifying details regarding the users of public, private, school, college, technical college, university, and state institutional libraries and library systems, supported in whole or in part by public funds or expending public funds, are confidential information.

Records which by themselves or when examined with other public records would reveal the identity of the library patron checking out or requesting an item from the library or using other library services are confidential information.

The confidential records do not include nonidentifying administrative and statistical reports of registration and circulation.

The confidential records may not be disclosed except to persons acting within the scope of their duties in the administration of the library or library system or persons authorized by the library patron to inspect his records, or in accordance with proper judicial order upon a finding that the disclosure of the records is necessary to protect public safety, to prosecute a crime, or upon a showing of good cause before the presiding Judge in a civil matter.

Section 60-4-20. As used in this chapter, the term 'registration records' includes any information which a library requires a patron to provide in order to become eligible to borrow books and other materials, and the term 'circulation records' includes all information which identifies the patrons borrowing particular books and other materials.

Section 60-4-30. Any person violating the provisions of Section 60-4-10 must upon conviction be fined not more than five hundred dollars or imprisoned for not more than thirty days for the first offense, must be fined not more than one thousand dollars or imprisoned for not more than sixty days for the second offense, and must be fined not more than two thousand dollars or imprisoned for not more than ninety days for the third or subsequent offense.

Definition

SECTION 2. Section 30-1-10 of the 1976 Code is amended to read:

"Section 30-1-10. For the purposes of Sections 30-1-10 to 30-1-140 'public records' means the records of meetings of all public agencies and includes all other records which by law are required to be kept or maintained by any public agency, and includes all documents containing information relating to the conduct of the public's business prepared, owned, used, or retained by any public agency, regardless of physical form or characteristics. Records such as income tax returns, medical records, scholastic records, adoption records, records related to registration, and circulation of library materials which contain names or other personally identifying details regarding the users of public, private, school, college, technical college, university, and state institutional libraries and library systems, supported in whole or in part by public funds or expending public funds, or records which reveal the identity of the library patron checking out or requesting an item from the library or using other library services, except nonidentifying administrative and statistical reports of registration and circulation, and other records which by law are required to be closed to the public are not considered to be made open to the public under the provisions of Sections 30-1-10 to 30-1-140, nor does the definition of public records include those records where it is shown that the public interest is best served by not disclosing them to the public. If necessary, security copies of closed or restricted records may be kept in the South Carolina Department of Archives and History, with the approval of the agency or political subdivision of origin and the Director of the Department of Archives and History. For purposes of records management closed and restricted records may be disposed of in accordance with the provisions of Sections 30-1-10 to 30-1-140 for the disposal of public records.

'Agency' means any state department, agency, or institution.

'Subdivision' means any political subdivision of the State.

'Archives' means the South Carolina Department of Archives and History.

'Director' means the Director of the Department of Archives and History."

Definition

SECTION 3. Subsection (c) of Section 3 of Act 593 of 1978 is amended to read:

"(c) 'Public record' includes all books, papers, maps, photographs, cards, tapes, recordings, or other documentary materials regardless of physical form or characteristics prepared, owned, used, in the possession of, or retained by a public body. Records such as income tax returns, medical records, hospital medical staff reports, scholastic records, adoption records, records related to registration, and circulation of library materials which contain names or other personally identifying details regarding the users of public, private, school, college, technical college, university, and state institutional libraries and library systems, supported in whole or in part by public funds or expending public funds, or records which reveal the identity of the library patron checking out or requesting an item from the library or using other library services, except nonidentifying administrative and statistical reports of registration and circulation, and other records which by law are required to be closed to the public are not considered to be made open to the public under the provisions of this act nor does the definition of public records include those records where the public body, by favorable public vote of three-fourths of the membership taken within fifteen working days after receipt of written request, concludes that the public interest is best served by not disclosing them. Nothing authorizes or requires the disclosure of records of the Board of Financial Institutions pertaining to applications and surveys for charters and branches of banks and savings and loan associations or surveys and examinations of the institutions required to be made by law."

Time effective

SECTION 4. This act shall take effect upon approval by the Governor.

Approved the 22nd day of May, 1985.

South Dakota   **Year of Passage: 1983**

Type of Law:

        __Part of state records access law
        x̲ Separate law specific to libraries
        __No law on confidentiality of library records

Types of Libraries covered:

        x̲ Public Libraries
        __Public Academic

_Public Schools
_Library Systems
_Private Libraries open to the public
_Any library using public funds

Covered Records:

x Patron Registration
x Circulation Records
_Use of Materials in Library
_Information Queries
_Requests for Materials
_Requests for Services

Law Defines Terms? _Yes _No

When information contained in library records may be released:

_With user consent
   [Consent must be in writing _Yes _No _Unclear]
**x Parent or guardian of minor seeks records of that
   minor**
_For library operation
x Pursuant to a court order or subpoena
_State Library request
_Education Department Request

Remarks: The records protected by this law are those that would
identify a patron.

Text of Law:

CHAPTER 154

(HB 1298)

CERTAIN PUBLIC LIBRARY RECORDS REQUIRED

TO BE KEPT CONFIDENTIAL—DESTRUCTION OF RECORDS

REQUIRED TO BE KEPT BY LAW PROHIBITED

AN ACT

ENTITLED, An Act to provide for the confidentiality of certain public
library records and maintenance of certain public records.

BE IT ENACTED BY THE LEGISLATURE OF THE STATE OF SOUTH DAKOTA:

Section 1. That chapter 14-2 be amended by adding thereto a new section to read as follows:

All public library records containing personally identifiable information are confidential. Any information contained in public library records may not be released except by court order or upon request of a parent of a child who is under eighteen years of age. As used in this section, "personally identifiable" means any information a library maintains that would identify a patron. Acts by library officers or employees in maintaining a check out system are not violations of this section.

Section 2. That Section 1-27-10 be amended to read as follows:

1-27-10. All records of public officials of this state required to be kept or maintained by law are the property of the state and may not be mutilated, destroyed, transferred, removed, or otherwise damaged or disposed of, in whole or in part, except as provided by law.

Signed March 15, 1983

Tennessee   **Year of Passage: 1988**

Type of Law:

    __Part of state records access law
    x Separate law specific to libraries
    __No law on confidentiality of library records

Types of Libraries covered:

    x Public Libraries
    x Public Academic
    x Public Schools
    x Library Systems
    x Private Libraries open to the public
    x Any library using public funds

Covered Records:

    x Patron Registration

x Circulation Records
x Use of Materials in Library
x Information Queries
x Requests for Materials
_Requests for Services

Law Defines Terms? x Yes _No

When information contained in library records may be released:

x With user consent
[Consent must be in writing x Yes _No _Unclear]
_Parent or guardian of minor seeks records of that minor
x For library operation
x Pursuant to a court order or subpoena
_State Library request
_Education Department Request

Text of Law:

HOUSE BILL NO. 2137

By Purcell, Cross, Moody, Turner, C. (Shelby), Williams

Substituted for: Senate Bill No. 2264

By Kyle

AN ACT to make confidential certain records maintained by libraries concerning library users and materials and to amend Tennessee Code Annotated, Title 10, Chapters 1,3,4, and 5.

BE IT ENACTED BY THE GENERAL ASSEMBLY OF THE STATE OF TENNESSEE:

SECTION 1. Tennessee Code Annotated, Title 10, Chapter 1,3,4 and 5 are amended by adding the following as a new part to each such chapter:

Section __. As used in this part unless the context otherwise requires:

(a) "Library" means a library that is open to the public and established or operated by the state, a county, city, town, school district or any other political subdivision of the state; or by a combination of governmental units or authorities; or by a university or community college; or any private library that is open to the public.

(b) "Library Record: means a document, record, or other method of storing information retained by a library that identifies a person as having requested or obtained specific information or materials from such library. "Library Record"

does not include nonidentifying material that may be retained for the purpose of studying or evaluating the circulation of library materials in general.

Section __.

(a) Except as provided in subsection (b) of this section, no employee of a library shall disclose any library record that identifies a person as having requested or obtained specific materials, information, or services or as having otherwise used such library. Such library records shall be considered an exception to the provisions of Tennessee code Annotated, Section 10-7-503.

(b) Library records may be disclosed under the following circumstances:

(1) Upon the written consent of the library user;

(2) Pursuant to the order of a court of competent jurisdiction; or

(3) When used to seek reimbursement for or the return of lost, stolen, misplaced or otherwise overdue library materials.

SECTION 2. This act shall take effect upon becoming a law, the public welfare requiring it.

Passed April 25, 1988. Approved by the Governor May 2, 1988.

Texas

Texas has no statute exempting library records from public inspection. However, under Texas' Open Records Law, information which is confidential under the Constitution is exempt. Under the Texas Open Records Decision No. 100 at 2-3(July 10, 1975) library circulation records are protected from disclosure under the First Amendment.

Utah   Year of Passage: 1992

Type of Law:

x Part of state records access law
__Separate law specific to libraries

_No law on confidentiality of library records

Types of Libraries covered:

_Public Libraries
_Public Academic
_Public Schools
_Library Systems
_Private Libraries open to the public
x Any library using public funds

Covered Records:

x Patron Registration
x Circulation Records
_Use of Materials in Library
_Information Queries
_Requests for Materials
_Requests for Services

Law Defines Terms? **x Yes** _No

When information contained in library records may be released:

_With user consent
[Consent must be in writing _Yes _No _Unclear]
_Parent or guardian of minor seeks records of that minor
_For library operation
_Pursuant to a court order or subpoena
_State Library request
_Education Department Request

Remarks: The Utah law has an appeals process carefully spelled out for those who might wish to view or to keep confidential any record covered by the Government Records Access and Management Act, II (GRAMA II).

*Text of Law:**

GOVERNMENT RECORDS ACCESS AND MANAGEMENT ACT, II

Effective July 1, 1992

PART 1. GENERAL PROVISIONS

63-2-101. Short title.

This chapter is known as the "Government Records Access and Management Act."

63-2-102. Legislative intent.

(1) In enacting this act, the Legislature recognizes two constitutional rights:

(a) the public's right of access to information concerning the conduct of the public's business; and

(b) the right of privacy in relation to personal data gathered by governmental entities.

(2) The Legislature also recognizes a public policy interest in allowing a government to restrict access to certain records, as specified in this chapter, for the public good.

(3) It is the intent of the Legislature to:

(a) promote the public's right of easy and reasonable access to unrestricted public records;

(b) specify those conditions under which the public interest in allowing restrictions on access to records may outweigh the public's interest in access.

(c) prevent abuse of confidentiality by governmental entities by permitting confidential treatment of records only as provided in this chapter;

(d) provide guidelines for both disclosure and restrictions on access to government records, which are based on the equitable weighing of the pertinent interests and which are consistent with nationwide standards of information practices;

(e) favor public access when, in the application of this act, countervailing interests are of equal weight; and

(f) establish fair and reasonable records management practices.

63-2-302. **Private records**.

(1) the following records are private:

. . .

(c) records of publicly funded libraries that when examined alone or with other records identify a patron; . . .

PART 6. ACCURACY OF RECORDS

63-2-601. Rights of individuals on whom data is maintained.

(1) (a) Each governmental entity shall file with the state archivist a statement explaining the purposes for which record series designated private or controlled are collected and used by that governmental entity.

(b) That statement is a public record.

(2) Upon request, each governmental entity shall explain to an individual:

(a) the reasons the individual is asked to furnish to the governmental entity information that could be classified private or controlled;

(b) the intended uses of the information; and

(c) the consequences for refusing to provide the information.

(3) A governmental entity may not use private or controlled records for purposes other than those given in the statement filed with the state archivist under Subsection (1) or for purposes other than those for which another governmental entity could use the record under Section 63-2-206.

. . .

PART 8. REMEDIES

63-2-801. Criminal penalties.

(1) (a) a public employee or other person who has lawful access to any private, controlled, or protected record under this chapter, and who intentionally discloses or provides a copy of a private, controlled, or protected record to any person knowing that such disclosure is prohibited, is guilty of a class B misdemeanor.

(b) It is a defense to prosecution under Subsection (1)(a) that the actor released private, controlled, or protected information in the reasonable belief that the disclosure of the information was necessary to expose a violation of law involving government corruption, abuse of office, or misappropriation of public funds or property.

(c) It is a defense to prosecution under Subsection (1)(a) that the record could have lawfully been released to the recipient if it had been properly classified.

(2) (a) A person who by false pretenses, bribery, or theft, gains access to or obtains a copy of any private, controlled, or protected record to which he is not legally entitled is guilty of a class B misdemeanor.

(b) No person shall be guilty under Subsection (2)(a) who receives the record, information, or copy after the fact and without prior knowledge of or participation in the false pretenses, bribery, or theft.

(3) A public employee who intentionally refuses to release a record

the disclosure of which the employee knows is required by law or by final unappealed order from a governmental entity, the records committee, or a court, is guilty of a class B misdemeanor.

. . .

63-2-804. Disciplinary action.

A governmental entity or political subdivision may take disciplinary action which may include suspension or discharge against any employee of the governmental entity or political subdivision who intentionally violates any provision of this chapter.

*The Utah Government Records Access and Management Act is a wide-ranging bill that encompasses the subject of access to information in all state agencies and institutions. The Act has many sections and pages. Here, only the intent of the bill, any pertinent definitions, the section dealing with library records, appeals, and penalties are reproduced. For further details of the bill, see the Utah Code.

Vermont   **Year of Passage: 1989**

Type of Law:

    x **Part of state records access law**
    x **Separate law specific to libraries**
    _No law on confidentiality of library records

Types of Libraries covered:

    x **Public Libraries**
    _Public Academic
    _Public Schools
    _Library Systems
    _Private Libraries open to the public
    x **Any library using public funds**

Covered Records:

    x **Patron Registration**
    x **Circulation Records**
    _Use of Materials in Library
    _Information Queries
    _Requests for Materials

_Requests for Services

Law Defines Terms? x Yes _No

When information contained in library records may be released:

_With user consent
[Consent must be in writing _Yes _No _Unclear]
_Parent or guardian of minor seeks records of that minor
_For library operation
_Pursuant to a court order or subpoena
_State Library request
_Education Department Request

Remarks: The bill passed to guarantee the confidentiality of certain library records does not contain exemptions. These may be found in the general records-access law of the state if any exemptions exist.

Text of Law:*

PUBLIC ACTS, 1989 SESSION

NO. 28. AN ACT RELATING TO PUBLIC LIBRARIES.(H. 137)

It is hereby enacted by the General Assembly of the State of Vermont:

Sec. 1. DECLARATION OF POLICY

The General Assembly hereby declares it to be the policy of the state of Vermont that free public libraries are essential to the general enlightenment of citizens in a democracy and that every citizen of the state of Vermont should have access to the educational, cultural, recreational, informational and research benefits of a free public library.

Sec. 2. 1 V.S.A. Section 317(b)(19) is added to read:

(19) Records relating to the identity of library patrons or the identity of library patrons in regard to the circulation of library materials.

Sec. 3. 12 V.S.A. Section 5782 is added to read:

Section 5782. LIBRARIES

A person employed by a library with or without compensation shall not be held personally liable for damages resulting from:

(1) information contained in any library materials; or

(2) library services provided to library patrons in the course of his or her duties.

. . .

As used in this chapter,

(1) "Municipality" means a town, city or incorporated village only and shall not include school districts, incorporated school or fire districts or any other governmental incorporated units.

(2) "Public Library" means any library established and maintained by a municipality or by a private association, corporation or group to provide basic library services free of charge to all residents of a municipality or a community and which receives its annual financial support in whole or in part from public funds.

. . .

*portions of the law were omitted because they relate to matters other than the confidentiality of library records.

Virginia   **Year of Passage: 1979**

Type of Law:

    <u>x</u> **Part of state records access law**
    _Separate law specific to libraries
    _No law on confidentiality of library records

Types of Libraries covered:

    _Public Libraries
    _Public Academic
    _Public Schools
    _Library Systems
    _Private Libraries open to the public
    _Any library using public funds

Covered Records:

    <u>x</u> **Patron Registration**
    <u>x</u> **Circulation Records**
    _Use of Materials in Library
    _Information Queries
    _Requests for Materials
    _Requests for Services

Law Defines Terms? __Yes __No

When information contained in library records may be released:

   __With user consent
   [Consent must be in writing __Yes __No __Unclear]
   __Parent or guardian of minor seeks records of that minor
   __For library operation
   __Pursuant to a court order or subpoena
   __State Library request
   __Education Department Request

Remarks: The bill says "Library records" and does not explain the phrase. Because the law is about public records, the inference can be made that libraries that are public agencies or part of a public agency are covered. The Virginia bill allows access to citizens of the state as well as to members of the media doing business in the state. When records are protected, this fact must be disclosed in writing to the requestor within a mandated time period. The public records law must be examined to determine exemptions.

Text of Law:*

ACTS OF THE GENERAL ASSEMBLY OF THE COMMONWEALTH OF VIRGINIA

SESSION 1979

CHAPTER 682

An Act to amend and reenact Section 2.1-342 of the Code of Virginia, relating to the Virginia Freedom of Information Act

[S 685]

Approved March 31, 1979

Be it enacted by the General Assembly of Virginia:

1. That Section 2.1-342 of the Code of Virginia is amended and reenacted as follows:

Section 2.1-342. Official records to be open to inspection; procedure for requesting records and responding to request; charges; exceptions to application of chapter.—(a)Except as otherwise specifically provided by law, all official records shall be open to inspection and copying by any citizens of this State during the regular office hours of the custodian of such records. Access to such records shall not be denied to any such citizen of this State, nor to representatives of newspapers and magazines with circulation in this State, and representatives of radio and television stations broadcasting in or into this State; provided that the custodian of such records shall take all necessary precautions for their preservation and safekeeping. Any public body covered under the provisions of this chapter shall make an initial response to citizens requesting records open to inspection within fourteen calendar days from the receipt of the request by the public body. Such citizen request shall designate the requested records with reasonable specificity. If the requested records or public body are excluded from the provisions of this chapter, the public body to which the request is directed shall within fourteen calendar days from the receipt of the request tender a written explanation as to why the records are not available to the requestor. Such explanation shall make specific reference to the applicable provisions of this chapter or other Code sections which make the requested records unavailable. In the event a determination of the availability of the requested records may not be made within the fourteen-calendar-day period, the public body to which the request is directed shall inform the requestor as such, and shall have an additional ten calendar days in which to make a determination of availability. A specific reference to this chapter by the requesting citizen in his records request shall not be necessary to invoke the time limits for response by the public body. The public body may make reasonable charges for the copying and search time expended in the supplying of such records; however, in no event shall such charges exceed the actual cost of the public body in supplying such records. Such charges for the supplying of requested records shall be estimated in advance at the request of the citizen.

(b) The following records are excluded from the provisions of this chapter:

. . .

(7)*Library records which can be used to identify both (i) any library patron who has borrowed material from a library and (ii) the material such patron borrowed.*

. . .

*Ellipses indicate the omission of parts of the law that do not deal with confidentiality of library records.

Washington   **Year of Passage: 1982**

Type of Law:

_Part of state records access law

_Separate law specific to libraries
_No law on confidentiality of library records

Types of Libraries covered:

_Public Libraries
_Public Academic
_Public Schools
_Library Systems
_Private Libraries open to the public
_Any library using public funds

Covered Records:

_Patron Registration
_Circulation Records
_Use of Materials in Library
_Information Queries
_Requests for Materials
_Requests for Services

Law Defines Terms? _Yes _No

When information contained in library records may be released:

_With user consent
 [Consent must be in writing _Yes _No _Unclear]
_Parent or guardian of minor seeks records of that minor
_For library operation
_Pursuant to a court order or subpoena
_State Library request
_Education Department Request

Text of Law:*

42.17.310 Certain personal and other records exempt. (1) The following are exempt from public inspection and copying:

. . .

(l)Any library record, the primary purpose of which is to maintain control of library materials, or to gain access to information, which discloses or could be used to disclose the identity of a library user.

...

*Portiions of the law that are not relevant to the topic at hand have been omitted.

West Virginia   **Year of Passage: 1990**

Type of Law:

        _Part of state records access law
        x Separate law specific to libraries
        _No law on confidentiality of library records

Types of Libraries covered:

        x Public Libraries
        _Public Academic
        _Public Schools
        _Library Systems
        _Private Libraries open to the public
        _Any library using public funds

Covered Records:

        x Patron Registration
        x Circulation Records
        _Use of Materials in Library
        _Information Queries
        _Requests for Materials
        _Requests for Services

Law Defines Terms? _Yes **x No**

When information contained in library records may be released:

        x With user consent
        [Consent must be in writing **x Yes** _No _Unclear]
        _Parent or guardian of minor seeks records of that minor
        x For library operation
        x Pursuant to a court order or subpoena
        _State Library request
        _Education Department Request

Text of law:

CHAPTER 156

(Com. Sub. for H.B. 4579—By Mr. Speaker, Mr. Chambers)

[Passed March 10, 1990; in effect ninety days from passage. Approved by the Governor.]

Confidential nature of certain library records.

(a) Circulation and similar records of any public library in this state which identify the user of library materials are not public records but shall be confidential and may not be disclosed except:

(1) To members of the library staff in the ordinary course of business;

(2) Upon written consent of the user of the library materials or the user's parents or guardian if the user is a minor or ward; or

(3) Upon appropriate court order or subpoena.

(b) Any disclosure authorized by subsection (a) of this section or any unauthorized disclosure of materials made confidential by that subsection (a) does not in any way destroy the confidential nature of that material, except for the purpose for which an authorized disclosure is made. A person disclosing material as authorized by subsection (a) of this section is not liable therefor. (1990, c. 156.)

Wisconsin   **Year of Passage: 1982**

Type of Law:

    x Part of state records access law
    _Separate law specific to libraries
    _No law on confidentiality of library records

Types of Libraries covered:

    _Public Libraries
    _Public Academic
    _Public Schools
    _Library Systems
    _Private Libraries open to the public
    x Any library using public funds

Covered Records:

x Patron Registration
x Circulation Records
__Use of Materials in Library
__Information Queries
__Requests for Materials
__Requests for Services

Law Defines Terms? __Yes **x No**

When information contained in library records may be released:

x With user consent
 [Consent must be in writing __Yes **x No** __Unclear]
__Parent or guardian of minor seeks records of that minor
x For library operation
x Pursuant to a court order or subpoena
__State Library request
__Education Department Request

*Text of Law:**

1981 Senate Bill 250 Date published: May 6, 1982

CHAPTER 335, Laws of 1981

The people of the state of Wisconsin represented in senate and assembly, do enact as follows:

. . .

SECTION 15. 43.30 of the statutes is created to read:

43.30 Public library circulation records. Records of any library which is in whole or in part supported by public funds, including the records of a public library system, indicating which of its documents or other materials have been loaned to or used by an identifiable individual may not be disclosed except to persons acting within the scope of their duties in the administration of the library or library system or persons authorized by the individual to inspect such records, or by order of a court of law.

. . .

*Portions of the bill unrelated to the confidentiality of library records have been omitted.

Wyoming   **Year of Passage: 1987**

Type of Law:

> **x Part of state records access law**
> _Separate law specific to libraries
> _No law on confidentiality of library records

Types of Libraries covered:

> **x Public Libraries**
> _Public Academic
> _Public Schools
> _Library Systems
> _Private Libraries open to the public
> _Any library using public funds

Covered Records:

> **x Patron Registration**
> **x Circulation Records**
> _Use of Materials in Library
> _Information Queries
> _Requests for Materials
> _Requests for Services

Law Defines Terms? _Yes **x No**

When information contained in library records may be released:

> _With user consent
> [Consent must be in writing _Yes _No _Unclear]
> **x Parent or guardian of minor seeks records of that minor**
> **x For library operation**
> _Pursuant to a court order or subpoena
> _State Library request
> _Education Department Request

Remarks: The law covers "library circulation and registration records," which implies public libraries. However it may also cover other types of libraries, for example those in public agencies and institutions.

Text of Law:*

[partial text from FOI Law of Wyoming]

16-4-203

(ix) Library circulation and registration records except as required for administration of the library or except as requested by a custodial parent or guardian to inspect the records of his minor child;

*In Wyoming, library circulation records are an exemption under the freedom of information law.

PART III

Library Policies

6
Sample Library Policy

Despite Constitutional and statutory protection, it is essential for all libraries to adopt a library policy to protect the privacy of their records. Such a policy, adopted by the library's governing body, establishes a nonarbitrary practice that can be used if a threat to privacy occurs. The policy also reminds staff of the importance of protecting that privacy and helps insure that the Constitutional and statutory laws are implemented.

I. AMERICAN LIBRARY ASSOCIATION

The American Library Association developed the following policy on confidentiality, procedures for implementing that policy, and a policy on governmental intimidation.[1]

POLICY ON CONFIDENTIALITY OF LIBRARY RECORDS[2]

The Council of the American Library Association strongly recommends that the responsible officers of each library, cooperative system, and consortium in the United States: (1.) Formally adopt a policy which specifically recognizes its circulation records and other records identifying the names of library users to be confidential in nature. (2.) Advise all librarians and library employees that such records shall not be made available to any agency of state, federal, or local government except pursuant to such process, order or subpoena as may be authorized under the authority of, and pursuant to, federal, state, or local law relating to civil, criminal, or administrative discovery procedures or legislative investigative power. (3.) Resist the issuance of enforcement of any such process, order, or subpoena until such time as a proper showing of good cause has been made in a court of competent jurisdiction.[3]

Adopted January 20, 1971; revised July 4, 1975, July 2, 1986, by the ALA Council.

[ISBN 8389-6082-0]

SUGGESTED PROCEDURES FOR IMPLEMENTING "POLICY ON CONFIDENTIALITY OF LIBRARY RECORDS"

When drafting local policies, libraries should consult with their legal counsel to insure these policies are based upon and consistent with applicable federal, state, and local law concerning the confidentiality of library records, the disclosure of public records, and the protection of individual privacy.

Suggested procedures include the following:

1. The library staff member receiving the request to examine or obtain information relating to circulation or other records identifying the names of library users will immediately refer the person making the request to the responsible officer of the institution, who shall explain the confidentiality policy.

2. The director, upon receipt of such process, order, or subpoena, shall consult with the appropriate legal officer assigned to the institution to determine if such process, order, or subpoena is in good form and if there is a showing of good cause for its issuance.

3. If the process, order, or subpoena is not in proper form or if good cause has not been shown, insistence shall be made that such defects be cured before any records are released. (The legal process requiring the production of circulation or other library records shall ordinarily be in the form of subpoena *"duces tecum"* [bring your records] requiring the responsible officer to attend court or the taking of his/her deposition and may require him/her to bring along certain designated circulation or other specified records.)

4. Any threats or unauthorized demands (i.e., those not supported by a process, order, or subpoena) concerning circulation and other records identifying the names of library users shall be reported to the appropriate legal officer of the institution.

5. Any problems relating to the privacy of circulation and other records identifying the names of library users which are not provided for above shall be referred to the responsible officer.

Adopted by the ALA Intellectual Freedom Committee, January 9, 1983; revised January 11, 1988.

POLICY ON GOVERNMENTAL INTIMIDATION

The American Library Association opposes any use of governmental prerogatives which leads to the intimidation of the individual or the citizenry from the exercise of free expression. ALA encourages resistance to such abuse of governmental power, and supports those against whom such governmental power has been employed.

Adopted February 2, 1973; amended July 1, 1981, by the ALA Council.

[ISBN 8389-5421-9]

II. SAMPLE POLICY

The following sample policy was developed in accordance with the Constitutional and legal principles explained in this workbook. It is recommended that this policy be posted at the circulation desk.

Library Policy on the Privacy of Library Records

I. The Library Board [Governing Body] hereby formally adopts a policy requiring the Library to observe Constitutional rules in the disclosure of personal information about individuals by specifically making confidential any personally identifiable patron or library user records including but not limited to circulation records, patron registration records, and reference requests except:
    (A) to the patron, or to the parent or guardian if the patron is a minor;
    (B) to any person with the informed written consent of the patron given at the time the disclosure is sought;
    (C) to any authorized person if the disclosure is necessary for the retrieval of overdue library materials or the recoupment of compensation for damaged or lost library materials; or
    (D) pursuant to a court order or subpoena authorizing such disclosure.
II. The agent for service of process in these matters shall be the Library Director.
III. Upon receipt of a court order or subpoena the Library will seek opinion of legal counsel as to validity of such court order or subpoena before complying.
IV. All library trustees, employees, volunteers, and friends shall comply with this policy; with all federal, state, and local laws or

regulations relating to the privacy of library records; and with relevant court decisions of the highest state and federal courts.

Notes

1. Reprinted by permission of the American Library Association.
2. See also ALA Policy Manual 54.16—Code Of Ethics, point #3: "Librarians must protect each user's right to privacy with respect to information sought or received, and materials consulted, borrowed, or acquired."
3. Point number three, above, means that upon receipt of such process, order, or subpoena, the library's officers will consult with their legal counsel to determine if such process, order, or subpoena is in proper form and if there is a showing of good cause of its issuance; if the process, order, or subpoena is not in proper form or if good cause has not been shown, they will insist that such defects be cured.

Appendix A

UNITED STATES SUPREME COURT OPINIONS: FIRST AMENDMENT AS AN ABSOLUTE PROHIBITION

The following excerpts from the majority opinions of the U. S. Supreme Court indicate that the full Court has consistently held that the First Amendment, despite its absolute language, is not to be interpreted as a total prohibition against any limitation on religion, expression, or the right of assembly or petition.

1897

The law is perfectly well settled that the first ten amendments to the Constitution, commonly known as the Bill of Rights, were not intended to lay down any novel principles of government, but simply to embody certain guaranties and immunities which had been inherited from our English ancestors, and which had from time immemorial been subject to certain well-recognized exceptions arising from the necessities of the case. In incorporating these principles into the fundamental law there was no intention of disregarding the exceptions, which continued to be recognized as if they had been formally expressed. Thus, the freedom of speech and of the press(art.1) does not permit the publication of libels, blasphemous or indecent articles, or other publications injurious to public morals or private reputation; the right of the people to keep and bear arms (art.2) is not infringed by laws prohibiting the carrying of concealed weapons; the provision that no person shall be twice put in jeopardy (art.5) does not prevent a second trial, if upon the first the jury failed to agree, or if the verdict was set aside upon the defendant's motion, *United States v. Ball*, 163 U.S. 662, 672; nor does the provision of the same article that no one shall be a witness against himself impair his obligation to testify, if prosecution against him be barred by the lapse of time, a pardon, or by statutory enactment. *Brown v. Walker*, 161 U.S. 591, and cases cited. Nor does the provision that an accused person shall be confronted with witnesses against him prevent the admission of dying declarations, or the depositions of witnesses who have died since the former trial. [*Robertson v. Baldwin*, 165 U.S. 275].

1920

. . . [W]e pass immediately to the contention and for the purpose of this case may concede it, that is, concede that the asserted freedom is natural and inherent, but it is not absolute, it is subject to restriction and limitation. And this we have decided. In *Schenck v. United States*, 249 U.S. 47, 52, we distinguished times and occasions and said that "the most stringent protection of free speech would not protect a man in falsely shouting fire in a theatre and causing a panic"; and in *Frohwerk v. United States*, 249 U.S. 204, 206, we said "that the First Amendment while prohibiting legislation against free speech as such cannot have been, and obviously was not, intended to give immunity for every possible use of language." See also, *Debs v. United States*, 249 U.S. 211; *Abrams v. United States*, 250 U.S. 616. In *Schaefer v. United States*, 251 U.S. 466, commenting on those cases and their contentions it was said that the curious spectacle of the Constitution of the United States being invoked to justify the activities of anarchy or of the enemies of the United States, and by a strange perversion of its precepts it was adduced against itself. And we did more than reject the contention, we forestalled all repetitions of it, and the contention in the case at bar is a repetition of it. It is a direct assault upon the statute of Minnesota, and a direct assertion in spite of the prohibition of the statute that one can by speech, teach or advocate that the citizens of the State should not aid or assist "the United States in prosecuting or carrying on war with the public enemies of the United States," and be protected by the Constitution of the United States. [*Gilbert v. Minnesota*, 254 U.S. 325].

1925

It is a fundamental principle, long established, that the freedom of speech and of the press which is secured by the Constitution does not confer an absolute right to speak or publish, without responsibility, whatever one may choose, or an unrestricted and unbridled license that gives immunity for every possible use of language and prevents the punishment of those who abuse this freedom. 2 Story on the Constitution, 5th ed., § 1580, p.634; *Robertson v. Baldwin*, 165 U.S. 275, 281; *Patterson v. Colorado*, 205 U.S. 454, 462; *Fox v. Washington*, 236 U.S. 273, 276; *Schenck v. United States*, 249 U.S. 47, 52; *Frohwerk v. United States*, 249 U.S. 204, 206; *Debs v. United States*, 249 U.S. 211, 213; *Schaefer v. United States*, 251 U.S. 466, 474; *Gilbert v. Minnesota*, 254 U.S. 325, 332; *Warren v. United States*, (C.C.A.) 183 Fed. 718, 721. Reasonably limited . . . this freedom is an inestimable privilege in a free government; without such limitation, it might become the scourge of the republic. [*Gitlow v. New York*, 268 U.S. 652 at 666].

1931

Liberty of speech, and of the press, is also not an absolute right, and the State may punish its abuse. [*Near v. Minnesota*, 283 U.S. 697 at 708].

1942

The rights of which our Constitution speaks have a more earthy quality. They are not absolutes to be exercised independently of other cherished privileges, protected by the same organic instrument. Conflicts in the exercise of rights arise, and the conflicting forces seek adjustments in the courts, as do these parties, claiming on the one side the freedom of religion, speech and the press, guaranteed by the Fourteenth Amendment, and on the other the right to employ the sovereign power explicitly reserved to the State by the Tenth Amendment to ensure orderly living, without which constitutional guarantees of civil liberties would be a mockery. Courts, no more than Constitutions, can intrude into the consciences of men or compel them to believe contrary to their faith or think contrary to their convictions; but courts are competent to adjudge the acts men do under color of a constitutional right, such as that of freedom of speech or of the press or the free exercise of religion, and to determine whether the claimed right is limited by other recognized powers, equally precious to mankind. So the mind and spirit of man remain forever free, while his actions rest subject to necessary accommodations to the competing needs of his fellows. [*Jones v. Opelika*, 316 U.S. 584 at 593-594].

1948

We recognize the importance of the exercise of a state's police power to minimize all incentives to crime, particularly in the field of sanguinary or salacious publications with their stimulation of juvenile delinquency. Although we are dealing with an aspect of a free press in its relation to public morals, the principles of unrestricted distribution of publications admonish us of the particular importance of a maintenance of standards of certainty in the field of criminal prosecutions for violations of statutory prohibitions against distribution. We do not accede to appellee's suggestion that the constitutional protection for a free press applies only to the exposition of ideas. The line between the informing and the entertaining is too elusive for the protection of that basic right. Everyone is familiar with instances of propaganda through fiction. What is one man's amusement, teaches another's doctrine. Though we can see nothing of any possible value to society in these magazines, they are as much entitled to the protection of free speech as the best of literature. Cf. *Hannegan v. Esquire*, 327 U.S. 146, 153, 158. They are equally subject to control if they are lewd, indecent, obscene or profane. [*Winters v. New York*, 333 U.S. 507 at 510].

1950

Although the First Amendment provides that Congress shall make no laws abridging the freedom of speech, press or assembly, it has long been established that those freedoms themselves are dependent upon the power of constitutional government to survive. If it is to survive it must have power to protect itself against unlawful conduct, and under some circumstances, against incitements to commit unlawful acts. Freedom of speech thus does not comprehend the right to speak on any subject at any time. The important question that came to this Court immediately after the First World War was not whether, but how far, the First Amendment permits the suppression of speech, which advocates conduct inimical to the public welfare. Some thought speech having a reasonable tendency to lead to such conduct might be punished. Justice Holmes and Brandeis took a different view. They thought that the greater danger to a democracy lies in the suppression of public discussion; that ideas and doctrines thought harmful or dangerous are best fought with words. Only, therefore, when force is very likely to follow an utterance before there is a chance for counter-argument to have effect may that utterance be punished or prevented. Thus, "the necessity which is essential to a valid restriction does not exist unless speech would produce, or is intended to produce, a clear and imminent danger of some substantive evil which the State [or Congress] constitutionally may seek to prevent. . . ." Mr. Justice Brandeis, concurring in *Whitney v. California*, 274 U.S. 357, 373. By this means they sought to convey the philosophy that under the First Amendment, the public has a right to every man's views and every man the right to speak them. Government may cut him off only when his views are no longer merely views but threaten, clearly and imminently, to ripen into conduct against which the public has a right to protect itself. [*American Communications Association v. Douds*, 339 U.S. 382 at 394-395].

1951

We pointed out in *Douds, supra,* that the basis of the First Amendment is the hypothesis that speech can rebut speech, propaganda, and that the free debate of ideas will result in the wisest government policies. It is for this reason that this Court has recognized the inherent value of free discourse. An analysis of the leading cases in this Court which have involved direct limitations on speech, however, will demonstrate that both the majority of the Court and the dissenters in particular cases have recognized that this is not an unlimited, unqualified right, but that the societal value of speech must, on occasion, be subordinated to other values and considerations. [*Dennis v. United States*, 341 U.S. 494 at 503].

The First and Fourteenth Amendments have never been treated as absolutes. Freedom of speech or press does not mean that one can talk or distribute where, when and how one chooses. Rights other than those of the advocates are involved. By adjustment of rights, we can have both full liberty of expression and an orderly life. [*Breard v. Alexandria*, 341 U.S. 622 at 642].

1953

The principles of the First Amendment are not to be treated as a promise that everyone with opinions or beliefs to express may gather around him at any public place and at any time a group for discussion or instruction. It is a *non sequitur* to say that First Amendment rights may not be regulated because they hold a preferred position in the hierarchy of the constitutional guarantees of the incidents of freedom. The Court has never so held and indeed has definitely indicated the contrary. [*Poulos v. New Hampshire*, 345 U.S. 395 at 405(1953)].

1957

The guaranties of freedom of expression in effect in 10 of the 14 States which by 1792 had ratified the Constitution, gave no absolute protection for every utterance. Thirteen of the 14 States provided for the prosecution of libel, and all of those States made either blasphemy or profanity, or both, statutory crimes. As early as 1712, Massachusetts made it criminal to publish "any filthy, obscene, or profane song, pamphlet, libel or mock sermon" in imitation or mimicking of religious services, Acts and Laws of the Province of Mass. Bay, c. CV, §8(1712). Mass. Bay Colony Charters & Laws 399 (1814). Thus profanity and obscenity were related offenses.

In light of this history, it is apparent that the unconditional phrasing of the First Amendment was not intended to protect every utterance. This phrasing did not prevent this Court from concluding that libelous utterances are not within the area of constitutionally protected speech. [*Roth v. United States*, 354 U.S. 476 at 482-83].

1961

In this perspective we consider the prior decisions of this Court, touching on the problem. Beginning over a third of a century ago in *Gitlow v. New York*, 268 U.S. 652(1925), they have consistently reserved for future decision possible situations in which the claimed First Amendment privilege might have to give way to the necessities of the public welfare. It has never been held that liberty of speech is absolute. Nor has it been suggested that all previous restraints on speech are invalid. On the contrary, in *Near v. Minnesota,* 283 U.S. 697, [at] 715-716(1931), Chief Justice Hughes, in discussing the classic legal statements concerning the immunity of the press from censorship, observed that the principle forbidding previous restraint "is stated too broadly, if every such restraint is deemed to be prohibited. . . . [T]he protection even as to previous restraint is not absolutely unlimited. But the limitation has been recognized only in exceptional cases." These included, the Chief Justice found, utterances creating "a hinderance" to the Government's war effort, and "actual obstruction to its recruiting service or the publication of the sailing date of transports or the number and location of troops." In addition, the Court said that "the primary requirements of decency may be enforced against obscene publications" and the "security of the community life may be protected against incitements to acts of violence and the overthrow by force of orderly government." Some years later, a unanimous Court, speaking through Mr. Justice Murphy, in *Chaplinsky v.*

New Hampshire, 315 U.S. 568, [at] 571-572(1942), held that there were "certain well-defined and narrowly limited classes of speech, the prevention and punishment of which have never been thought to raise any Constitutional problem. These include the lewd and obscene, the profane, the libelous, and the insulting or 'fighting' words— those which by their very utterance inflict injury or tend to incite an immediate breach of the peace." Thereafter, as we have mentioned, in *Joseph Burstyn, Inc., v. Wilson, supra*, we found motion pictures to be within the guarantees of the First and Fourteenth Amendments, but we added that this was "not the end of our problem. It does not follow that the Constitution requires absolute freedom to exhibit every motion picture of every kind at all times and all places." At p.502. Five years later, in *Roth v. United States*, 354 U.S. 476, 483(1957), we held that "in light of . . . history, it is apparent that the unconditional phrasing of the First Amendment was not intended to protect every utterance." Even those in dissent there found that "Freedom of expression can be suppressed if, and to the extent that it is so closely brigaded with illegal action as to be an inseparable part of it." *Id.*, at 514. And, during the same Term, in *Kingsley Books, Inc. v. Brown*, 354 U.S. 436, [at] 441(1957)after characterizing *Near v. Minnesota*, *supra*, as "one of the landmark opinions" in this area, we took notice that *Near* "left no doubts that 'Liberty of speech, and of the press, is also not an absolute right . . . the protection even as to previous restraint is not absolutely unlimited. . . . The judicial angle of vision," we said there, "in testing the validity of a statute like §22-a [New York's injunctive remedy against certain forms of obscenity] is 'the operation and effect of the statute in substance.'" And as if to emphasize the point involved here, we added that "The phrase 'prior restraint' is not a self-wielding sword. Nor can it serve as a talisman test." Even as recently as our last Term we again observed the principle, albeit in an allied area, that the State possesses some measure of power "to prevent the distribution of obscene matter." *Smith v. California*, 361 U.S. 147, [at] 155(1959). [*Times Film Corp. v. Chicago*, 365 U.S. 43 at 47-49].

1965

The rights of free speech and assembly, while fundamental in our democratic society, still do not mean that everyone with opinions or beliefs to express may address a group at any public place at any time. The constitutional guarantee of liberty implies the existence of an organized society, without which liberty itself would be lost in the excesses of anarchy. The control of travel on the streets is a clear example of governmental responsibility to insure this necessary order. A restriction in that relation, designed to promote the public convenience in the interest of all, and not susceptible to abuses of discriminatory application, cannot be disregarded by the attempted exercise of some civil right which, in other circumstances, would be entitled to protection. One would not be justified in ignoring the familiar red light because this was thought to be a means of social protest. Nor could one, contrary to traffic regulations, insist upon a street meeting in the middle of Times Square at the rush hour as a form of freedom of speech or assembly. Governmental authorities have the duty and responsibility to keep their streets open and available for movement. A group of demonstrators could not insist upon the right to cordon off a street, or entrance to a public or private building, and allow no one to pass who did not agree to listen to their exhortations. [*Cox v. Louisiana*, 379 U.S. 536 at 554-555(1965)].

1969

These later decisions have fashioned the principle that the constitutional guarantees of free speech and free press do not permit a State to forbid or proscribe advocacy of the use of force or of law violation except where such advocacy is directed to inciting or producing such action. [*Brandenberg v. Ohio*, 395 U.S. 444 at 447].

1971

This does not end the inquiry, of course, for the First and Fourteenth Amendments have never been thought to give absolute protection to every individual to speak whenever or wherever he pleases, or to use any form of address in any circumstances that he chooses. [*Cohen v. California*, 403 U.S. 15 at 19].

Appendix B

U.S. FREEDOM OF INFORMATION ACT

(5 U.S.C. Sec. 552)

(a) Each agency shall make available to the public information as follows:

    (1) Each agency shall separately state and currently publish in the Federal Register for the guidance of the public—

        (A) descriptions of its central and field organization and the established places at which, the employees (and in the case of a uniformed service, the members) from whom, and the methods whereby, the public may obtain information, make submittals or requests, or obtain decisions;

        (B) statements of the general course and method by which its functions are channeled and determined, including the nature and requirements of all formal and informal procedures available;

        (C) rules of procedure, descriptions of forms available or the places at which forms may be obtained, and instructions as to the scope and contents of all papers, reports, or examinations;

        (D) substantive rules of general applicability adopted as authorized by law, and statements of general policy or interpretations of general applicability formulated and adopted by the agency; and

        (E) each amendment, revision, or repeal of the foregoing.

Except to the extent that a person has actual and timely notice of the terms thereof, a person may not in any manner be required to resort to, or be adversely affected by, a matter required to be published in the Federal Register and not so published. For the purpose of this paragraph, matter reasonably available to the class of persons affected thereby is deemed published in the Federal Register when incorporated by reference therein with the approval of the Director of the Federal Register.

(2) Each agency, in accordance with published rules, shall make available for public inspection and copying—

(A) final opinions, including concurring and dissenting opinions, as well as orders, made in the adjudication of cases;

(B) those statements of policy and interpretations which have been adopted by the agency and are not published in the Federal Register; and

(C) administrative staff manuals and instructions to staff that affect a member of the public; unless the materials are promptly published and copies offered for sale. To the extent required to prevent a clearly unwarranted invasion of personal privacy, an agency may delete identifying details when it makes available or publishes an opinion, statement of policy, interpretation, or staff manual or instruction. However, in each case the justification for the deletion shall be explained fully in writing. Each agency shall also maintain and make available for public inspection and copying current indexes providing identifying information for the public as to any matter issued, adopted, or promulgated after July 4, 1967, and required by this paragraph to be made available or published. Each agency shall promptly publish, quarterly or more frequently, and distribute (by sale or otherwise) copies of each index or supplements thereto unless it determines by order published in the Federal Register that the publication would be unnecessary and impracticable, in which case the agency shall nonetheless provide copies of such index on request at a cost not to exceed the direct cost of duplication. A final order, opinion, statement of policy, interpretation, or staff manual or instruction that affects a member of the public may be relied on, used, or cited as precedent by an agency against a party other than an agency only if—

      (i) it has been indexed and either made available or published as provided by this paragraph; or

     (ii) the party has actual and timely notice of the terms thereof.

(3) Except with respect to the records made available under paragraphs (1) and (2) of this subsection, each agency, upon any request for records which

    (A) reasonably describes such records and

    (B) is made in accordance with published rules stating the time, place, fees (if any), and procedures to be followed, shall make the records promptly available to any person.

(4)(A)(i)   In order to carry out the provisions of this section, each agency shall promulgate regulations, pursuant to notice and receipt of public comment, specifying the schedule of fees applicable to the processing of requests under this section and establishing procedures and guidelines for determining when such fees should be waived or reduced. Such schedule shall conform to the guidelines which shall be promulgated, pursuant to notice and receipt of public comment, by the Director of the Office of Management and Budget and which shall provide for a uniform schedule of fees for all agencies.

    (ii) Such agency regulations shall provide that—

        (I)   fees shall be limited to reasonable standard charges for document search, duplication, and review, when records are requested for commercial use;

       (II)   fees shall be limited to reasonable standard charges for document duplication when records are not sought for commercial use and the request is made by an educational or noncommercial scientific institution, whose purpose is scholarly or scientific research; or a representative of the news media; and

      (III) for any request not described in (I) or (II), fees shall be limited to reasonable standard charges for document search and duplication.

    (iii) Documents shall be furnished without any charge or at a charge reduced below the fees established under clause (ii) if disclosure of the information is in the public interest because it is likely to contribute significantly to public understanding of the operations or activities of the government and is not primarily in the commercial interest of the requester.

(iv) Fee schedules shall provide for the recovery of only the direct costs of search, duplication, or review. Review costs shall include only the direct costs incurred during the initial examination of a document for the purposes of determining whether the documents must be disclosed under this section and for the purposes of withholding any portions exempt from disclosure under this section. Review costs may not include any costs incurred in resolving issues of law or policy that may be raised in the course of processing a request under this section. No fee may be charged by any agency under this section -

(I)   if the costs of routine collection and processing of the fee are likely to equal or exceed the amount of the fee; or

(II) for any request described in clause (ii) (II) or (III) of this subparagraph for the first two hours of search time or for the first one hundred pages of duplication.

(v) No agency may require advance payment of any fee unless the requester has previously failed to pay fees in a timely fashion, or the agency has determined that the fee will exceed $250.

(vi) Nothing in this subparagraph shall supersede fees chargeable under a statute specifically providing for setting the level of fees for particular types of records.

(vii)In any action by a requester regarding the waiver of fees under this section, the court shall determine the matter de novo: Provided, That the court's review of the matter shall be limited to the record before the agency.

(B) On complaint, the district court of the United States in the district in which the complainant resides, or has his principal place of business, or in which the agency records are situated, or in the District of Columbia, has jurisdiction to enjoin the agency from withholding agency records and to order the production of any agency records improperly withheld from the complainant. In such a case the court shall determine the matter de novo, and may examine the contents of such agency records in camera to determine whether such records or any part thereof shall be withheld under any of the exemptions set forth in subsection (b) of this section, and the burden is on the agency to sustain its action.

(C) Notwithstanding any other provision of law, the defendant shall serve an answer or otherwise plead to any complaint made under this subsection within thirty days after service upon the defendant of the pleading in which such complaint is made, unless the court otherwise directs for good cause shown.

((D)Repealed. Pub. L. 98-620, title IV, Sec. 402(2), Nov. 8, 1984, 98 Stat. 3357.)

(E) The court may assess against the United States reasonable attorney fees and other litigation costs reasonably incurred in any case under this section in which the complainant has substantially prevailed.

(F) Whenever the court orders the production of any agency records improperly withheld from the complainant and assesses against the United States reasonable attorney fees and other litigation costs, and the court additionally issues a written finding that the circumstances surrounding the withholding raise questions whether agency personnel acted arbitrarily or capriciously with respect to the withholding, the Special Counsel shall promptly initiate a proceeding to determine whether disciplinary action is warranted against the officer or employee who was primarily responsible for the withholding. The Special Counsel, after investigation and consideration of the evidence submitted, shall submit his findings and recommendations to the administrative authority of the agency concerned and shall send copies of the findings and recommendations to the officer or employee or his representative. The administrative authority shall take the corrective action that the Special Counsel recommends.

(G) In the event of noncompliance with the order of the court, the district court may punish for contempt the responsible employee, and in the case of a uniformed service, the responsible member.

(5) Each agency having more than one member shall maintain and make available for public inspection a record of the final votes of each member in every agency proceeding.

(6)(A) Each agency, upon any request for records made under paragraph (1), (2), or (3) of this subsection, shall—

    (i) determine within ten days (excepting Saturdays, Sundays, and legal public holidays) after the receipt of any such request whether to comply with such request and shall immediately notify the person making such request of such determination and the reasons therefor, and of the right of such person to appeal to the head of the agency any adverse determination; and

    (ii) make a determination with respect to any appeal within twenty days (excepting Saturdays, Sundays, and legal public holidays) after the receipt of such appeal. If on appeal the denial of the request for records is in whole or in part upheld, the agency shall notify the person making such request of the provisions for judicial review of that determination under paragraph (4) of this subsection.

(B) In unusual circumstances as specified in this subparagraph, the time limits prescribed in either clause (i) or clause (ii) of subparagraph (A) may be extended by written notice to the person making such request setting forth the reasons for such extension and the date on which a determination is expected to be dispatched. No such notice shall specify a date that would result in an extension for more than ten working days. As used in this subparagraph, 'unusual circumstances' means, but only to the extent reasonably necessary to the proper processing of the particular request—

    (i) the need to search for and collect the requested records from field facilities or other establishments that are separate from the office processing the request;

    (ii) the need to search for, collect, and appropriately examine a voluminous amount of separate and distinct records which are demanded in a single request; or

    (iii) the need for consultation, which shall be conducted with all practicable speed, with another agency having a substantial interest in the determination of the request or among two or more components of the agency having substantial subject-matter interest therein.

(C) Any person making a request to any agency for records under paragraph (1), (2), or (3) of this subsection shall be deemed to have exhausted his administrative remedies with respect to such request if the agency fails to comply with the applicable time limit provisions of this paragraph. If the Government can show exceptional circumstances exist and that the agency is exercising due diligence in responding to the request, the court may retain jurisdiction and allow the agency additional time to complete its review of the records. Upon any determination by an agency to comply with a request for records, the records shall be made promptly available to such person making such request. Any notification of denial of any request for records under this subsection shall set forth the names and titles or positions of each person responsible for the denial of such request.

(b) This section does not apply to matters that are—

(1)(A) specifically authorized under criteria established bby an Executive order to be kept secret in the interest of national defense or foreign policy and (B) are in fact properly classified pursuant to such Executive order;

(2) related solely to the internal personnel rules and practices of an agency;

(3) specifically exempted from disclosure by statute (other than section 552b of this title), provided that such statute

(A) requires that the matters be withheld from the public in such a manner as to leave no discretion on the issue, or

(B) establishes particular criteria for withholding or refers to particular types of matters to be withheld;

(4) trade secrets and commercial or financial information obtained from a person and privileged or confidential;

(5) inter-agency or intra-agency memorandums or letters which would not be available by law to a party other than an agency in litigation with the agency;

(6) personnel and medical files and similar files the disclosure of which would constitute a clearly unwarranted invasion of personal privacy;

(7) records or information compiled for law enforcement purpos-

es, but only to the extent that the production of such law enforcement records or information

(A) could reasonably be expected to interfere with enforcement proceedings,

(B) would deprive a person of a right to a fair trial or an impartial adjudication,

(C) could reasonably be expected to constitute an unwarranted invasion of personal privacy,

(D) could reasonably be expected to disclose the identity of a confidential source, including a State, local, or foreign agency or authority or any private institution which furnished information on a confidential basis, and, in the case of a record or information compiled by criminal law enforcement authority in the course of a criminal investigation or by an agency conducting a lawful national security intelligence investigation, information furnished by a confidential source,

(E) would disclose techniques and procedures for law enforcement investigations or prosecutions, or would disclose guidelines for law enforcement investigations or prosecutions if such disclosure could reasonably be expected to risk circumvention of the law, or

(F) could reasonably be expected to endanger the life or physical safety of any individual;

(8) contained in or related to examination, operating, or condition reports prepared by, on behalf of, or for the use of an agency responsible for the regulation or supervision of financial institutions; or

(9) geological and geophysical information and data, including maps, concerning wells.

Any reasonably segregable portion of a record shall be provided to any person requesting such record after deletion of the portions which are exempt under this subsection.

(c)(1) Whenever a request is made which involves access to records described in subsection (b)(7)(A) and—

(A) the investigation or proceeding involves a possible violation of criminal law; and

(B) there is reason to believe that

(i) the subject of the investigation or proceeding is not aware of its pendency, and

(ii) disclosure of the existence of the records could reasonably be expected to interfere with enforcement proceedings, the agency may, during only such time as that circumstance continues, treat the records as not subject to the requirements of this section.

(2) Whenever informant records maintained by a criminal law enforcement agency under an informant's name or personal identifier are requested by a third party according to the informant's name or personal identifier, the agency may treat the records as not subject to the requirements of this section unless the informant's status as an informant has been officially confirmed.

(3) Whenever a request is made which involves access to records maintained by the Federal Bureau of Investigation pertaining to foreign intelligence or counterintelligence, or international terrorism, and the existence of the records is classified information as provided in subsection (b)(1), the Bureau may, as long as the existence of the records remains classified information, treat the records as not subject to the requirements of this section.

(d) This section does not authorize withholding of information or limit the availability of records to the public, except as specifically stated in this section. This section is not authority to withhold information from Congress.

(e) On or before March 1 of each calendar year, each agency shall submit a report covering the preceding calendar year to the Speaker of the House of Representatives and President of the Senate for referral to the appropriate committees of the Congress. The report shall include—

(1) the number of determinations made by such agency not to comply with requests for records made to such agency under subsection (a) and the reasons for each such determination;

(2) the number of appeals made by persons under subsection (a)(6), the result of such appeals, and the reason for the action upon each appeal that results in a denial of information;

(3) the names and titles or positions of each person responsible for the denial of records requested under this section, and the number of instances of participation for each;

(4) the results of each proceeding conducted pursuant to subsection (a)(4)(F), including a report of the disciplinary action taken against the officer or employee who was primarily responsible for improperly withholding records or an explanation of why disciplinary action was not taken;

(5) a copy of every rule made by such agency regarding this section;

> (6) a copy of the fee schedule and the total amount of fees collected by the agency for making records available under this section; and
>
> (7) such other information as indicates efforts to administer fully this section.

The Attorney General shall submit an annual report on or before March 1 of each calendar year which shall include for the prior calendar year a listing of the number of cases arising under this section, the exemption involved in each case, the disposition of such case, and the cost, fees, and penalties assessed under subsections (a)(4)(E), (F), and (G). Such report shall also include a description of the efforts undertaken by the Department of Justice to encourage agency compliance with this section.

(f) For purposes of this section, the term 'agency' as defined in section 551(1) of this title includes any executive department, military department, Government corporation, Government controlled corporation, or other establishment in the executive branch of the Government (including the Executive Office of the President), or any independent regulatory agency.

SHORT TITLE: This section is popularly known as the 'Freedom of Information Act.'

Appendix C

U.S. SUPREME COURT ON THE CONSTITUTIONAL RIGHT TO PRIVACY

The following are excerpts from majority as well as dissenting opinions.

1891

The single question presented by this record is whether, in a civil action for an injury to the person, the court, on application of the defendant, and in advance of the trial, may order the plaintiff, without his or her consent, to submit to a surgical examination as to the extent of the injury sued for. We concur with the circuit court in holding that it had no legal right or power to make and enforce such an order.

No right is held more sacred, or is more carefully guarded by the common law, than the right of every individual to the possession and control of his own person, free from all restraint or interference of others, unless by clear and unquestionable authority of law [*Union Pacific Railroad Co. v. Botsford*, 141 U.S. 250 at 251].

1928

The makers of our Constitution undertook to secure conditions favorable to the pursuit of happiness. They recognized the signifi-cance of man's spiritual nature, of his feelings and of his intellect.

They knew that only a part of the pain, pleasure and satisfactions of life are to be found in material things. They sought to protect Americans in their beliefs, their thoughts, their emotions and their sensations. They conferred, as against the Government, the right to be let alone—the most comprehensive of rights and the right most valued by civilized man. [*Olmstead v. United States*, 277 U.S. 438, 478(Brandeis, J., dissenting)].

1951

This makes the constitutionality of Alexandria's ordinance turn upon a balancing of the conveniences between some householders' desire for privacy and the publisher's right to distribute publications in the precise way that those soliciting for him think brings the best results. The issue brings into collision the rights of the hospitable housewife, peering on Monday morning around her chained door with those of Mr. Breard's courteous, well-trained but possibly persistent solicitor, offering a bargain on culture, and information through a joint subscription to Satevepost, Pic and Today's Woman. Behind the housewife are many housewives and home-owners in the towns where Green River ordinances offer their aid. Behind Mr. Breard are "Keystone" with an annual business of $5,000,000 in subscriptions and periodicals with their use of house-to-house canvassing to secure subscribers for their valuable publications, together with other housewives who desire solicitors to offer them the opportunity and remind and help them, at their doors, to subscribe for publications.

Subscriptions may be made by anyone interested in receiving the magazines without the annoyances of house-to-house canvassing. We think those communities that have found these methods of sale obnoxious may control them by ordinance. It would be, it seems to us, a misuse of the great guarantees of free speech and free press to use those guarantees to force a community to admit the solicitors of publications to the home premises of its residents. We see no abridgement of the principles of the First Amendment in this ordinance. [*Breard v. Alexandria*, 341 U.S. 622 at 644-645].

1951

Liberty in the constitutional sense must mean more than freedom from unlawful governmental restraint; it must include privacy as well, if it is to be a repository of freedom. The right to be let alone is indeed the beginning of all freedom . . . To think what one wishes are important aspects of the constitutional right to be let alone. [*Public*

Utilities Commission v. Pollak, 343 U.S. 451 at 467 (Douglas, J. dissenting)].

1958

This Court has recognized the vital relationship between freedom to associate and privacy in one's association. . . . [*NAACP v. Alabama*, 357 U.S. 449 at 462].

1959

Against this background two protections emerge from the broad constitutional proscription of official invasion. The first of these is the right to be secure from intrusion into personal privacy, the right to shut the door on officials of the state unless their entry is under proper authority of law. The second, and intimately related protection, is self protection: the right to resist unauthorized entry which has as its design the securing of information to fortify the coercive power of the state against the individual information which may be used to effect a further deprivation of life or liberty or property. [*Frank v. Maryland*, 359 U.S. 360 at 365].

1961

This notion of privacy is not drawn from the blue. It emanates from the totality of the constitutional scheme under which we live. . . Can there be any doubt that a Bill of Rights that in time of peace bars soldiers from being quartered in a home "without the consent of the Owner" [Third Amendment] should also bar the police from investigating the intimacies of the marriage relation? The idea of allowing the State that leeway is congenial only to a totalitarian regime. [*Poe v. Ullman*, 367 U.S. 497 at 521 (Douglas, J. dissenting)].

1965

Various [constitutional] guarantees create zones of privacy. [*Griswold v. Connecticut*, 381 U.S. 479 at 484].

1968

The Fourth Amendment provides that "the right of the people to be secure in their persons, houses, papers, and effects, against unreasonable searches and seizures, shall not be violated. . . ." This inestimable right of personal security belongs as much to the citizen on the streets or our cities as to the homeowner closeted in his study to dispose of his secret affairs.

1969

For also fundamental is the right to be free, except in very limited circumstance, from unwanted government intrusions into one's privacy. [*Stanley v. Georgia*, 394 U.S. 557 at 564].

1973

This right of privacy, whether it be founded in the Fourteenth Amendment's concept of personal liberty and restrictions upon state action, as we feel it is, or, as the District Court determined, in the Ninth Amendment's reservation of rights to the people, is broad enough to encompass a woman's decision whether or not to terminate her pregnancy. [*Roe v. Wade*, 410 U.S. 113 at 153].

Appendix D

FEDERAL PRIVACY ACT: CONGRESSIONAL FINDINGS AND STATEMENT OF PURPOSE

(a) The Congress finds that—
 (1) the privacy of an individual is directly affected by the collection, maintenance, use, and dissemination of personal information by Federal agencies;
 (2) the increasing use of computers and sophisticated information technology, while essential to the efficient operations of the Government, has greatly magnified the harm to individual privacy that can occur from any collection, maintenance, use, or dissemination of personal information;
 (3) the opportunities for an individual to secure employment, insurance, and credit, and his right to due process, and other legal protections are endangered by the misuse of certain information systems;
 (4) the right to privacy is a personal and fundamental right protected by the Constitution of the United States; and
 (5) in order to protect the privacy of individuals identified in information systems maintained by Federal agencies, it is necessary and proper for the Congress to regulate the collection, maintenance, use, and dissemination of information by such agencies.
(b) The purpose of this Act is to provide certain safeguards for an

individual against an invasion of personal privacy by requiring
Federal agencies, except as otherwise provided by law, to—

(1) permit an individual to determine what records pertaining to
him are collected, maintained, used, or disseminated by such
agencies;

(2) permit an individual to prevent records pertaining to him
obtained by such agencies for a particular purpose from being
used or made available for another purpose without his
consent;

(3) permit an individual to gain access to information pertaining
to him in Federal agency records, to have a copy made of all or
any portion thereof, and to correct or amend such records;

(4) collect, maintain, use, or disseminate any record of identifiable personal information in a manner that assures that such
action is for a necessary and lawful purpose, that the information is current and accurate for its intended use, and that
adequate safeguards are provided to prevent misuse of such
information;

(5) permit exemptions from the requirements with respect to
records provided in this Act only in those cases where there is
an important public policy need for such exemption as has
been determined by specific statutory authority; and

(6) be subject to civil suit for any damages which occur as a result
of willful or intentional action which violates any individual's
rights under this Act.

Appendix E

VIDEO AND LIBRARY PRIVACY PROTECTION ACT
OF 1988

S.2361
100TH CONGRESS
2ND SESSION

To amend title 18, United States Code, to preserve personal privacy with respect to the rental, purchase, or delivery of video tapes or similar audio visual materials and the use of library materials or services.

IN THE SENATE OF THE UNITED STATES
MAY 10 (LEGISLATIVE DAY, MAY 9), 1988

Mr. LEAHY (for himself, Mr. GRASSLEY, Mr. SIMON, and Mr. SIMPSON) introduced the following bill; which was read twice and referred to the Committee on the Judiciary

A BILL

To amend title 18, United States Code, to preserve personal privacy with respect to the rental, purchase, or delivery of video tapes or similar audio visual materials and the use of library materials or services.

Be it enacted by the Senate and House of Representatives of the United States of America in Congress assembled, SECTION 1.SHORT TITLE.

This Act may be cited as the "Video and Library Privacy Protection Act of 1988."

SEC. 2.CHAPTER 121 AMENDMENT.

(a)   IN GENERAL.—Chapter 121 of title 18, United States Code, is amended—
    (1)   by redesignating section 2710 as section 2711;

and

    (2)   by inserting after section 2709 the following:

S 2710. Wrongful disclosure of video tape rental or sale records and library records.

"(a)   DEFINITIONS.—For purposes of this section—
    "(1)   the term 'patron' means any individual who requests or receives—
        "(A)   services within a library; or
        "(B)   books or other materials on loan from a library;
    "(2)   the term 'consumer' means any renter, purchases, or subscriber of goods or services from a video tape service provider;
    "(3)   the term 'library' means an institution which operates as a public library or serves as a library for any university, school, or college;
    "(4)   the term 'ordinary course of business' means only debt collection activities and the transfer of ownership;
    "(5)   the term 'personally identifiable information' includes information which identifies a person as having requested or obtained specific materials or services from a video tape service provider or library; and
    "(6)   the term 'video tape provider' means any person, engaged in the business of rental, sale or delivery of pre-recorded video cassette tapes or similar audio visual materials.
"(b)   VIDEO TAPE RENTAL AND SALE RECORDS.—(1) A video tape service provider who knowingly discloses, to any person, personally identifiable information concerning any consumer of

such provider shall be liable to the aggrieved person for the relief provided in subsection (d)

"(2) A video tape service provider may disclose personally identifiable information concerning any consumer—

"(A) to the consumer;

"(B) to any person with the informed, written consent of the consumer given at the time the disclosure is sought;

"(C) to a law enforcement agency pursuant to a court order authorizing such disclosure if—

"(i)   the consumer is given reasonable notice, by the law enforcement agency, of the court proceeding relevant to the issuance of the court order and is afforded the opportunity to appear and contest the claim of the law enforcement agency; and

"(ii) such law enforcement agency offers clear and convincing evidence that the subject of the information is reasonably suspected of engaging in criminal activity and the information sought is highly probative and material to the case;

"(D) to any person if the disclosure is solely of the names and addresses of consumers and if—

"(i)   the video tape service provider has provided the consumer with the opportunity, in a writing separate from any rental, sales, or subscription agreement, to prohibit such disclosure; and

"(ii) the disclosure does not reveal, directly or indirectly, the title, description, or subject matter of any video tapes or other audio visual material;

"(E) to any person if the disclosure is incident to the ordinary course of business of the video tape service provider; or

"(F) pursuant to an court order, in a civil proceeding upon a showing of compelling need for the information that cannot be accommodated by any other means, if—

"(i)   the consumer is given reasonable notice, by the person seeking the disclosure, of the court proceeding relevant to the issuance of the court order; and

"(ii) the consumer is afforded the opportunity to appear and contest the claim of the person seeking the disclosure.

"(c) LIBRARY RECORDS.—(1) Any library which knowingly discloses, to any person, personally identifiable information concerning any patron of such institution shall be liable to the aggrieved person for the relief provided in subsection (d).

"(2) A library may disclose personally identifiable information concerning any patron—

"(A) to the patron;

"(B) to any person with the informed written consent of the patron given at the time the disclosure is sought.

"(C) to a law enforcement agency pursuant to a court order authorizing such disclosure if -

"(i) the patron is given reasonable notice, by the law enforcement agency, of the court proceeding relevant to the issuance of the court order and is afforded the opportunity to appear and contest the claim of the law enforcement agency; and

"(ii) such law enforcement agency offers clear and convincing evidence that the subject of the information is reasonably suspected of engaging in criminal activity and that the information sought is highly probative and material to the case;

"(D) to any person if the disclosure is solely of the names and addresses of patrons and if -

"(i) the library has provided the patron with a written statement which affords the patron the opportunity to prohibit such disclosure; and

"(ii) the disclosure does not reveal, directly or indirectly, the title, description, or subject matter of any library materials borrowed or services utilized by the patron;

"(E) to any authorized person if the disclosure is necessary for the retrieval of overdue library materials or the recoupment of compensation for damaged or lost library materials; or

"(F) pursuant to a court order, in a civil proceeding upon a showing of compelling need for the information that cannot be accommodated by any other means, if -

"(i) the patron is given reasonable notice, by the person seeking the disclosure, of the court proceeding relevant to the issuance of the court order; and

"(ii) the patron is afforded the opportunity to appear

and contest the claim of the person seeking the disclosure.

If an order is granted pursuant to subparagraph (C) or (F), the court shall impose appropriate safeguards against unauthorized disclosure.

"(d) CIVIL ACTION.—(1) Any person aggrieved by any act of a person in violation of this section may bring a civil action in a United State district court.

"(2) The court may award -

"(A) actual damages but not less than liquidated damages in an amount of $2,500;

"(B) punitive damages;

"(C) reasonable attorneys' fees and other litigation costs reasonably incurred; and

"(D) such other preliminary and equitable relief as the court determines to be appropriate.

"(3) No action may be brought under this subsection unless such action is begun within 2 years from the date of the act complained of or the date of discovery.

"(4) No liability shall result from lawful disclosure permitted by this section.

"(e) Personally identifiable information obtained in any manner other than as provided in this section shall not be received in evidence in any trial, hearing, arbitration, or other proceeding in or before any court, grand jury, department, officer, agency, regulatory body, legislative committee, or other authority of the United States, a State, or a political subdivision of a State.

"(f) DESTRUCTION OF OLD RECORDS. - A person subject to this section shall destroy personally identifiable information as soon as practicable, but no later than one year from the date the information is no longer necessary for the purpose for which it was collected and there are no pending requests or orders for access to such information under subsections (b)(2) or (c)(2) or pursuant to a court order.

"(g) SELECTION OF A FORUM. - Nothing in this section shall limit rights of consumer or patrons otherwise provided under State or local law. A Federal court shall, in accordance with section 1738 of title 28, United States Code, give preclusive effect to the decision of any State or local court or agency in an action brought by a consumer or patron under a State or local law similar to this section. A decision of a Federal court under this section shall preclude any action under a State or local law similar to this section.".

(b)   CLERICAL AMENDMENT. - The table of sections at the beginning of chapter 121 of title 18, United States Code, is amended -

(1)   in the item relating to section 2710, by striking out "2710" and inserting "2711" in lieu thereof;

and

(2)   by inserting after the item relating to section 2709 the following new item:

"2710. Wrongful disclosure of video tape rental or sale record and library records."

Appendix F

PUBLIC LAW 100-618

WRONGFUL DISCLOSURE OF VIDEO TAPE RENTAL OR SALE RECORDS

(a) Definitions.—For purposes of this section—
    (1) the term 'consumer' means any renter, purchaser, or subscriber of goods or services from a video tape service provider;
    (2) the term 'ordinary course of business' means only debt collection activities, order fulfillment, request processing, and the transfer of ownership;
    (3) the term 'personally identifiable information' includes information which identifies a person as having requested or obtained specific video materials or services from a video tape service provider; and
    (4) the term 'video tape service provider' means any person, engaged in the business, in or affecting interstate or foreign commerce, of rental, sale, or delivery of prerecorded video cassette tapes or similar audio visual materials, or any person or other entity to whom a disclosure is made under subparagraph (D) or (E) of subsection (b)(2), but only with respect to the information contained in the disclosure.
(b) Video Tape Rental and Sale Records.—(1) A video tape service provider who knowingly discloses, to any person, personally identifiable information concerning any consumer of such provid-

er shall be liable to the aggrieved person for the relief provided in subsection (d).

(2) A video tape service provider may disclose personally identifiable information concerning any consumer—

(A) to the consumer;

(B) to any person with the informed, written consent of the consumer given at the time the disclosure is sought;

(C) to a law enforcement agency pursuant to a warrant issued under the Federal Rules of Criminal Procedure, an equivalent State warrant, a grand jury subpoena, or a court order;

(D) to any person if the disclosure is solely of the names and addresses of consumers and if—

(i) the video tape service provider has provided the consumer with the opportunity, in a clear and conspicuous manner, to prohibit such disclosure; and

(ii) the disclosure does not identify the title, description, or subject matter of any video tapes or other audio visual material; however, the subject matter of such materials may be disclosed if the disclosure is for the exclusive use of marketing goods and services directly to the consumer;

(E) to any person if the disclosure is incident to the ordinary course of business of the video tape service provider; or

(F) pursuant to a court order, in a civil proceeding upon a showing of compelling need for the information that cannot be accommodated by any other means, if—

(i) the consumer is given reasonable notice, by the person seeking the disclosure, of the court proceeding relevant to the issuance of the court order; and

(ii) the consumer is afforded the opportunity to appear and contest the claim of the person seeking the disclosure. If an order is granted pursuant to subparagraph (C) or (F), the court shall impose appropriate safeguards against unauthorized disclosure.

(3) Court orders authorizing disclosure under subparagraph (C) shall issue only with prior notice to the consumer and only if the law enforcement agency shows that there is probable cause to believe that the records or other information sought are relevant to a legitimate law enforcement inquiry. In the case of a State government authority, such a court order shall not issue if prohibited by the law of such State. A court

issuing an order pursuant to this section, on a motion made promptly by the video tape service provider, may quash or modify such order if the information or records requested are unreasonably voluminous in nature or if compliance with such order otherwise would cause an unreasonable burden on such provider.

(c) Civil Action.—(1) Any person aggrieved by any act of a person in violation of this section may bring a civil action in a United States district court.

(2) The court may award—

    (A) actual damages but not less than liquidated damages in an amount of $2,500;

    (B) punitive damages;

    (C) reasonable attorneys' fees and other litigation costs reasonably incurred; and

    (D) such other preliminary and equitable relief as the court determines to be appropriate.

(3) No action may be brought under this subsection unless such action is begun within 2 years from the date of the act complained of or the date of discovery.

(4) No liability shall result from lawful disclosure permitted by this section.

(d) Personally Identifiable Information.—Personally identifiable information obtained in any manner other than as provided in this section shall not be received in evidence in any trial, hearing, arbitration, or other proceeding in or before any court, grand jury, department, officer, agency, regulatory body, legislative committee, or other authority of the United States, a State, or a political subdivision of a State.

(e) Destruction of Old Records.—A person subject to this section shall destroy personally identifiable information as soon as practicable, but no later than one year from the date the information is no longer necessary for the purpose for which it was collected and there are no pending requests or orders for access to such information under subsection (b)(2) or (c)(2) or pursuant to a court order.

(f) Preemption.—The provisions of this section preempt only the provisions of State or local law that require disclosure prohibited by this section.

(Added Pub. L. 100-618, Sec. 2(a)(2), Nov. 5, 1988, 102 Stat. 3195.)

Index